TEACHER'S PET PUBLICATIONS

PUZZLE PACK
for
The Outsiders

based on the book by
S. E. Hinton

Written by
William T. Collins

© 2005 Teacher's Pet Publications
All Rights Reserved

The materials in this packet are copyrighted
by Teacher's Pet Publications, Inc.

These pages may be duplicated by the purchaser
for use in the purchaser's own classroom.

Copying any of these materials and distributing them
for any other purpose is a violation of the copyright laws.

© 2005 Teacher's Pet Publications, Inc.
www.tpet.com

INTRODUCTION
If you already own the LitPlan for this title, this Puzzle Pack will refresh your Unit Resource Materials and Vocabulary Resource Materials sections plus give you additional materials you can substitute into the tests. If you do not already have a complete LitPlan, these pages will give you some supplemental materials to use with your own plan. There are two main groups of materials: one set for unit words (such as characters' names, symbols, places, etc.) and one set for vocabulary words associated with the book.

WORD LIST
There is a word list for both the unit words and the vocabulary words. These lists show you which words are being used in the materials and the clues or definitions being used for those words. You may want to give students a word list with clues/definitions to help them, or you may want students to only have a word list (without clues/definitions) if you want them to work a little harder. Both are available for duplication. The word lists can also be your "calling key" for the bingo games.

FILL IN THE BLANK AND MATCHING
There are 4 each of the fill in the blank and matching worksheets for both the unit and vocabulary words. These pages can be used either as extra worksheets for students or as objective parts of a unit test. They can be done individually if students need extra help or as a whole class activity to review the material covered.

MAGIC SQUARES
The magic squares not only reinforce the material covered but also work on reasoning and math skills. Many teachers have told us that their students really enjoy doing these!

WORD SEARCH PUZZLES
The word search words go in all directions, as indicated on your answer keys. Two of the word search puzzles have the clues listed rather than the words. This makes the puzzle a little more difficult, but it reinforces the material better. Two word search puzzles have words only for students who find the clue puzzles too difficult.

CROSSWORD PUZZLES
Both unit and vocabulary word sections have 4 crossword puzzles.

BINGO CARDS
There are 32 individual bingo cards for the unit words and 32 individual bingo cards for the vocabulary words. You can use your word list as a "call list," calling the words at random and marking them off of your list as you go, or you could use the flash cards by cutting them apart and drawing the words at random from a hat (or box or whatever). To make a better review, you might ask for the definition and spelling of each word as you call it out–or you could call out the definitions and have students tell you the words they need to look for on the puzzle.

JUGGLE LETTERS
The vocabulary juggle letter game is intended to help students learn the spellings of the words. One sheet has the definitions listed on it as an extra help for students who need it or to reinforce the definitions if you choose to do so.

FLASH CARDS
We've included a set of vocabulary flash cards you can duplicate, cut, and fold for your students. Some teachers make a few sets for general use by the class; others make a set for each student. Some teachers duplicate them for each student and have the students cut & fold their own. You can cut out just the words and put them in a hat, have each student pick out one word and write the definition and a sentence for that word. Students then swap words and papers, with the next student adding a sentence of his own under the last one. You can have students swap as many times as you like. Each time the student will read the sentences written prior to his own and then add a sentence. You can cut out the words and definitions separately and play "I Have; Who Has?" Each student in the room draws a word and definition. The first student says, "I have (the name of the word). Who has the definition?" The student with the definition reads it then says, "I have (the name of the vocabulary word she has). Who has the definition?" The round continues until all words and definitions have been given.

The Outsiders Word List

No.	Word	Clue/Definition
1.	ARM	Dally injured his getting Johnny out.
2.	BARBECUE	Kind of sandwiches Johnny ate
3.	BLADE	Slang for knife
4.	BLOOD	Red body fluid
5.	BLUE	Mustang color
6.	BOB	Johnny killed him.
7.	BOOK	Johnny's gift to Pony; Gone With the Wind
8.	BOTTLE	Pony broke the end off one and threatened Socs.
9.	BROTHERS	Darry, Soda and Pony, for example
10.	CHERRY	She became a Greaser spy.
11.	CHURCH	Hide-out that caught on fire
12.	CIGARETTES	Pony smoked them
13.	COKE	Cherry threw hers into Dally's face.
14.	DALLAS	Police shot him
15.	DARRY	Pony's eldest brother
16.	DEAD	Condition of Bob, Dally and Johnny
17.	DOUBLE	Nightly _____
18.	FIGHT	Another name for rumble
19.	FIRE	The church caught on _____.
20.	FOUNTAIN	Pony was almost drowned in it.
21.	FROST	Poet Robert
22.	FUN	Soda fought for this reason.
23.	GALLANT	Johnny liked this land of southern gentlemen.
24.	GOLDEN	What Johnny wanted Pony to stay
25.	GOOD	Johnny's note said that there is still _____ in the world.
26.	GREASERS	East-end gang
27.	GUN	Dally pointed an unloaded one at the police.
28.	HAIRCUT	Getting one upset Pony because he lost his trademark.
29.	HINTON	Author
30.	HOSPITAL	Place were Johnny died
31.	JACKET	Gang symbol
32.	JOHNNY	He killed Bob and saved the children.
33.	JUDGE	He acquitted Pony.
34.	KNIFE	Johnny's murder weapon
35.	LATE	Darry hit Pony because he was ___.
36.	LOT	Pony and Johnny fell asleep in the empty _____.
37.	MARCIA	Cherry's Soc sidekick
38.	MOTHER	Johnny rejected his _____'s visit.
39.	MOUNTAIN	Jay's _____
40.	MUSTANG	Blue Soc car
41.	NEWSPAPER	Place for printed accounts of news
42.	OUTSIDERS	The _____; book title
43.	PAUL	Holden; He started a rumble
44.	PONYBOY	The narrator
45.	PRIDE	Reason Darry fought; Pony's hair symbolized his
46.	RANDY	Tried to call off the big rumble
47.	RINGS	Bob wore these on his fingers.
48.	RUMBLE	Fight
49.	SMOKE	Firefighters get it; ____ inhalation
50.	SOCS	The West-end gang
51.	SODAPOP	Middle brother

The Outsiders Word List Continued

No. Word	Clue/Definition
52. SPY	Cherry is one for the Greasers.
53. THEME	Pony is assigned to write one.
54. TIM	Hard-fighter Shepards first name
55. TRAIN	Transportation to Windrixville
56. TURF	Slang for area
57. TWO	He fought because everyone else did--to conform; ___-Bit
58. WINSTON	Dally's last name

The Outsiders Fill In The Blanks 1

1. The narrator
2. Poet Robert
3. Bob wore these on his fingers.
4. Pony was almost drowned in it.
5. The church caught on _____.
6. Holden; He started a rumble
7. Cherry is one for the Greasers.
8. Transportation to Windrixville
9. Johnny liked this land of southern gentlemen.
10. Tried to call off the big rumble
11. Place for printed accounts of news
12. Middle brother
13. Mustang color
14. He killed Bob and saved the children.
15. Hard-fighter Shepards first name
16. Pony's eldest brother
17. Red body fluid
18. Hide-out that caught on fire
19. Condition of Bob, Dally and Johnny
20. Johnny killed him.

The Outsiders Fill In The Blanks 1 Answer Key

PONYBOY	1. The narrator
FROST	2. Poet Robert
RINGS	3. Bob wore these on his fingers.
FOUNTAIN	4. Pony was almost drowned in it.
FIRE	5. The church caught on _____.
PAUL	6. Holden; He started a rumble
SPY	7. Cherry is one for the Greasers.
TRAIN	8. Transportation to Windrixville
GALLANT	9. Johnny liked this land of southern gentlemen.
RANDY	10. Tried to call off the big rumble
NEWSPAPER	11. Place for printed accounts of news
SODAPOP	12. Middle brother
BLUE	13. Mustang color
JOHNNY	14. He killed Bob and saved the children.
TIM	15. Hard-fighter Shepards first name
DARRY	16. Pony's eldest brother
BLOOD	17. Red body fluid
CHURCH	18. Hide-out that caught on fire
DEAD	19. Condition of Bob, Dally and Johnny
BOB	20. Johnny killed him.

Copyrighted

The Outsiders Fill In The Blanks 2

_____ 1. Bob wore these on his fingers.
_____ 2. She became a Greaser spy.
_____ 3. Jay's _____
_____ 4. Johnny killed him.
_____ 5. Johnny's note said that there is still _____ in the world.
_____ 6. Nightly _____
_____ 7. Pony was almost drowned in it.
_____ 8. Darry, Soda and Pony, for example
_____ 9. East-end gang
_____ 10. Kind of sandwiches Johnny ate
_____ 11. Tried to call off the big rumble
_____ 12. Condition of Bob, Dally and Johnny
_____ 13. Pony is assigned to write one.
_____ 14. What Johnny wanted Pony to stay
_____ 15. Place were Johnny died
_____ 16. Mustang color
_____ 17. The church caught on _____.
_____ 18. Cherry is one for the Greasers.
_____ 19. Transportation to Windrixville
_____ 20. Police shot him

The Outsiders Fill In The Blanks 2 Answer Key

RINGS	1.	Bob wore these on his fingers.
CHERRY	2.	She became a Greaser spy.
MOUNTAIN	3.	Jay's _____
BOB	4.	Johnny killed him.
GOOD	5.	Johnny's note said that there is still _____ in the world.
DOUBLE	6.	Nightly _____
FOUNTAIN	7.	Pony was almost drowned in it.
BROTHERS	8.	Darry, Soda and Pony, for example
GREASERS	9.	East-end gang
BARBECUE	10.	Kind of sandwiches Johnny ate
RANDY	11.	Tried to call off the big rumble
DEAD	12.	Condition of Bob, Dally and Johnny
THEME	13.	Pony is assigned to write one.
GOLDEN	14.	What Johnny wanted Pony to stay
HOSPITAL	15.	Place were Johnny died
BLUE	16.	Mustang color
FIRE	17.	The church caught on _____.
SPY	18.	Cherry is one for the Greasers.
TRAIN	19.	Transportation to Windrixville
DALLAS	20.	Police shot him

The Outsiders Fill In The Blanks 3

1. Johnny rejected his _____'s visit.
2. Johnny killed him.
3. Johnny's murder weapon
4. He killed Bob and saved the children.
5. Cherry is one for the Greasers.
6. Dally pointed an unloaded one at the police.
7. Kind of sandwiches Johnny ate
8. East-end gang
9. Pony broke the end off one and threatened Socs.
10. Getting one upset Pony because he lost his trademark.
11. Bob wore these on his fingers.
12. He fought because everyone else did--to conform; ___-Bit
13. Slang for knife
14. Nightly _____
15. Dally injured his getting Johnny out.
16. Darry hit Pony because he was ___.
17. Johnny's note said that there is still _____ in the world.
18. Johnny's gift to Pony; Gone With the Wind
19. Blue Soc car
20. Darry, Soda and Pony, for example

The Outsiders Fill In The Blanks 3 Answer Key

MOTHER	1. Johnny rejected his _____'s visit.
BOB	2. Johnny killed him.
KNIFE	3. Johnny's murder weapon
JOHNNY	4. He killed Bob and saved the children.
SPY	5. Cherry is one for the Greasers.
GUN	6. Dally pointed an unloaded one at the police.
BARBECUE	7. Kind of sandwiches Johnny ate
GREASERS	8. East-end gang
BOTTLE	9. Pony broke the end off one and threatened Socs.
HAIRCUT	10. Getting one upset Pony because he lost his trademark.
RINGS	11. Bob wore these on his fingers.
TWO	12. He fought because everyone else did--to conform; ___-Bit
BLADE	13. Slang for knife
DOUBLE	14. Nightly _____
ARM	15. Dally injured his getting Johnny out.
LATE	16. Darry hit Pony because he was ___.
GOOD	17. Johnny's note said that there is still _____ in the world.
BOOK	18. Johnny's gift to Pony; Gone With the Wind
MUSTANG	19. Blue Soc car
BROTHERS	20. Darry, Soda and Pony, for example

The Outsiders Fill In The Blanks 4

1. Slang for area
2. He fought because everyone else did--to conform; ___-Bit
3. Dally injured his getting Johnny out.
4. Johnny's gift to Pony; Gone With the Wind
5. Cherry threw hers into Dally's face.
6. Slang for knife
7. Place for printed accounts of news
8. Johnny's murder weapon
9. Nightly _____
10. Gang symbol
11. Johnny liked this land of southern gentlemen.
12. Dally pointed an unloaded one at the police.
13. Middle brother
14. Cherry is one for the Greasers.
15. He acquitted Pony.
16. Pony's eldest brother
17. The church caught on _____.
18. Author
19. Firefighters get it; ____ inhalation
20. Kind of sandwiches Johnny ate

The Outsiders Fill In The Blanks 4 Answer Key

TURF	1.	Slang for area
TWO	2.	He fought because everyone else did--to conform; ___-Bit
ARM	3.	Dally injured his getting Johnny out.
BOOK	4.	Johnny's gift to Pony; Gone With the Wind
COKE	5.	Cherry threw hers into Dally's face.
BLADE	6.	Slang for knife
NEWSPAPER	7.	Place for printed accounts of news
KNIFE	8.	Johnny's murder weapon
DOUBLE	9.	Nightly _____
JACKET	10.	Gang symbol
GALLANT	11.	Johnny liked this land of southern gentlemen.
GUN	12.	Dally pointed an unloaded one at the police.
SODAPOP	13.	Middle brother
SPY	14.	Cherry is one for the Greasers.
JUDGE	15.	He acquitted Pony.
DARRY	16.	Pony's eldest brother
FIRE	17.	The church caught on _____.
HINTON	18.	Author
SMOKE	19.	Firefighters get it; ____ inhalation
BARBECUE	20.	Kind of sandwiches Johnny ate

The Outsiders Matching 1

___ 1. FOUNTAIN   A. Johnny's note said that there is still _____ in the world.
___ 2. HINTON   B. Gang symbol
___ 3. PAUL   C. Holden; He started a rumble
___ 4. JUDGE   D. Slang for knife
___ 5. TWO   E. He acquitted Pony.
___ 6. DEAD   F. Hide-out that caught on fire
___ 7. BARBECUE   G. Fight
___ 8. GOOD   H. Author
___ 9. BOB   I. Slang for area
___10. MUSTANG   J. Firefighters get it; ____ inhalation
___11. CHURCH   K. Johnny killed him.
___12. HOSPITAL   L. Condition of Bob, Dally and Johnny
___13. ARM   M. What Johnny wanted Pony to stay
___14. TURF   N. Cherry threw hers into Dally's face.
___15. GOLDEN   O. He killed Bob and saved the children.
___16. RANDY   P. Middle brother
___17. JACKET   Q. Dally injured his getting Johnny out.
___18. RUMBLE   R. Kind of sandwiches Johnny ate
___19. JOHNNY   S. Blue Soc car
___20. SMOKE   T. Tried to call off the big rumble
___21. COKE   U. Place were Johnny died
___22. BLADE   V. Pony's eldest brother
___23. DARRY   W. Pony was almost drowned in it.
___24. SODAPOP   X. Place for printed accounts of news
___25. NEWSPAPER   Y. He fought because everyone else did--to conform; ___-Bit

The Outsiders Matching 1 Answer Key

W - 1. FOUNTAIN A. Johnny's note said that there is still _____ in the world.
H - 2. HINTON B. Gang symbol
C - 3. PAUL C. Holden; He started a rumble
E - 4. JUDGE D. Slang for knife
Y - 5. TWO E. He acquitted Pony.
L - 6. DEAD F. Hide-out that caught on fire
R - 7. BARBECUE G. Fight
A - 8. GOOD H. Author
K - 9. BOB I. Slang for area
S - 10. MUSTANG J. Firefighters get it; ____ inhalation
F - 11. CHURCH K. Johnny killed him.
U - 12. HOSPITAL L. Condition of Bob, Dally and Johnny
Q - 13. ARM M. What Johnny wanted Pony to stay
I - 14. TURF N. Cherry threw hers into Dally's face.
M - 15. GOLDEN O. He killed Bob and saved the children.
T - 16. RANDY P. Middle brother
B - 17. JACKET Q. Dally injured his getting Johnny out.
G - 18. RUMBLE R. Kind of sandwiches Johnny ate
O - 19. JOHNNY S. Blue Soc car
J - 20. SMOKE T. Tried to call off the big rumble
N - 21. COKE U. Place were Johnny died
D - 22. BLADE V. Pony's eldest brother
V - 23. DARRY W. Pony was almost drowned in it.
P - 24. SODAPOP X. Place for printed accounts of news
X - 25. NEWSPAPER Y. He fought because everyone else did--to conform; ___-Bit

The Outsiders Matching 2

___ 1. COKE	A. Another name for rumble
___ 2. PAUL	B. Darry, Soda and Pony, for example
___ 3. BOB	C. Place for printed accounts of news
___ 4. BOTTLE	D. Kind of sandwiches Johnny ate
___ 5. GALLANT	E. Fight
___ 6. HOSPITAL	F. He fought because everyone else did--to conform; ___-Bit
___ 7. HAIRCUT	G. Johnny liked this land of southern gentlemen.
___ 8. BLADE	H. Holden; He started a rumble
___ 9. GUN	I. Pony and Johnny fell asleep in the empty _____.
___10. FIRE	J. Cherry threw hers into Dally's face.
___11. GREASERS	K. Slang for knife
___12. GOOD	L. Place were Johnny died
___13. LATE	M. He killed Bob and saved the children.
___14. DEAD	N. Johnny's gift to Pony; Gone With the Wind
___15. FIGHT	O. Johnny killed him.
___16. BROTHERS	P. Darry hit Pony because he was ___.
___17. DALLAS	Q. Police shot him
___18. BOOK	R. The church caught on _____.
___19. RANDY	S. Johnny's note said that there is still _____ in the world.
___20. JOHNNY	T. Dally pointed an unloaded one at the police.
___21. LOT	U. Condition of Bob, Dally and Johnny
___22. RUMBLE	V. East-end gang
___23. BARBECUE	W. Pony broke the end off one and threatened Socs.
___24. NEWSPAPER	X. Tried to call off the big rumble
___25. TWO	Y. Getting one upset Pony because he lost his trademark.

The Outsiders Matching 2 Answer Key

J - 1. COKE   A. Another name for rumble
H - 2. PAUL   B. Darry, Soda and Pony, for example
O - 3. BOB   C. Place for printed accounts of news
W - 4. BOTTLE   D. Kind of sandwiches Johnny ate
G - 5. GALLANT   E. Fight
L - 6. HOSPITAL   F. He fought because everyone else did--to conform; ___-Bit
Y - 7. HAIRCUT   G. Johnny liked this land of southern gentlemen.
K - 8. BLADE   H. Holden; He started a rumble
T - 9. GUN   I. Pony and Johnny fell asleep in the empty _____.
R -10. FIRE   J. Cherry threw hers into Dally's face.
V -11. GREASERS   K. Slang for knife
S -12. GOOD   L. Place were Johnny died
P -13. LATE   M. He killed Bob and saved the children.
U -14. DEAD   N. Johnny's gift to Pony; Gone With the Wind
A -15. FIGHT   O. Johnny killed him.
B -16. BROTHERS   P. Darry hit Pony because he was ___.
Q -17. DALLAS   Q. Police shot him
N -18. BOOK   R. The church caught on _____.
X -19. RANDY   S. Johnny's note said that there is still _____ in the world.
M -20. JOHNNY   T. Dally pointed an unloaded one at the police.
I -21. LOT   U. Condition of Bob, Dally and Johnny
E -22. RUMBLE   V. East-end gang
D -23. BARBECUE   W. Pony broke the end off one and threatened Socs.
C -24. NEWSPAPER   X. Tried to call off the big rumble
F -25. TWO   Y. Getting one upset Pony because he lost his trademark.

The Outsiders Matching 3

___ 1. TURF   A. Firefighters get it; ____ inhalation
___ 2. BLOOD   B. Author
___ 3. SMOKE   C. Fight
___ 4. COKE   D. Dally pointed an unloaded one at the police.
___ 5. MOTHER   E. Dally's last name
___ 6. MARCIA   F. Darry, Soda and Pony, for example
___ 7. OUTSIDERS   G. The _____; book title
___ 8. RUMBLE   H. Cherry's Soc sidekick
___ 9. NEWSPAPER   I. Slang for area
___10. HOSPITAL   J. He acquitted Pony.
___11. WINSTON   K. Place for printed accounts of news
___12. BROTHERS   L. Pony was almost drowned in it.
___13. BOOK   M. Johnny killed him.
___14. HINTON   N. Place were Johnny died
___15. ARM   O. Holden; He started a rumble
___16. JACKET   P. Gang symbol
___17. BOB   Q. Pony broke the end off one and threatened Socs.
___18. FOUNTAIN   R. Johnny rejected his _____'s visit.
___19. PAUL   S. Red body fluid
___20. BOTTLE   T. Cherry threw hers into Dally's face.
___21. BLUE   U. Dally injured his getting Johnny out.
___22. JUDGE   V. Condition of Bob, Dally and Johnny
___23. GUN   W. Johnny's gift to Pony; Gone With the Wind
___24. FUN   X. Mustang color
___25. DEAD   Y. Soda fought for this reason.

The Outsiders Matching 3 Answer Key

I -	1. TURF	A.	Firefighters get it; ____ inhalation
S -	2. BLOOD	B.	Author
A -	3. SMOKE	C.	Fight
T -	4. COKE	D.	Dally pointed an unloaded one at the police.
R -	5. MOTHER	E.	Dally's last name
H -	6. MARCIA	F.	Darry, Soda and Pony, for example
G -	7. OUTSIDERS	G.	The _____; book title
C -	8. RUMBLE	H.	Cherry's Soc sidekick
K -	9. NEWSPAPER	I.	Slang for area
N -	10. HOSPITAL	J.	He acquitted Pony.
E -	11. WINSTON	K.	Place for printed accounts of news
F -	12. BROTHERS	L.	Pony was almost drowned in it.
W -	13. BOOK	M.	Johnny killed him.
B -	14. HINTON	N.	Place were Johnny died
U -	15. ARM	O.	Holden; He started a rumble
P -	16. JACKET	P.	Gang symbol
M -	17. BOB	Q.	Pony broke the end off one and threatened Socs.
L -	18. FOUNTAIN	R.	Johnny rejected his _____'s visit.
O -	19. PAUL	S.	Red body fluid
Q -	20. BOTTLE	T.	Cherry threw hers into Dally's face.
X -	21. BLUE	U.	Dally injured his getting Johnny out.
J -	22. JUDGE	V.	Condition of Bob, Dally and Johnny
D -	23. GUN	W.	Johnny's gift to Pony; Gone With the Wind
Y -	24. FUN	X.	Mustang color
V -	25. DEAD	Y.	Soda fought for this reason.

The Outsiders Matching 4

___ 1. GREASERS   A. Pony is assigned to write one.
___ 2. TURF   B. Cherry is one for the Greasers.
___ 3. RUMBLE   C. Author
___ 4. WINSTON   D. Fight
___ 5. BLOOD   E. Red body fluid
___ 6. KNIFE   F. Darry hit Pony because he was ___.
___ 7. PONYBOY   G. Dally's last name
___ 8. COKE   H. Darry, Soda and Pony, for example
___ 9. SMOKE   I. Holden; He started a rumble
___10. HAIRCUT   J. Place were Johnny died
___11. SPY   K. Kind of sandwiches Johnny ate
___12. BARBECUE   L. Cherry's Soc sidekick
___13. BROTHERS   M. Firefighters get it; ____ inhalation
___14. HINTON   N. Getting one upset Pony because he lost his trademark.
___15. CHURCH   O. Johnny killed him.
___16. DOUBLE   P. The narrator
___17. THEME   Q. East-end gang
___18. HOSPITAL   R. Nightly _____
___19. OUTSIDERS   S. He fought because everyone else did--to conform; ___-Bit
___20. LATE   T. Cherry threw hers into Dally's face.
___21. MARCIA   U. He killed Bob and saved the children.
___22. JOHNNY   V. Slang for area
___23. BOB   W. The _____; book title
___24. PAUL   X. Johnny's murder weapon
___25. TWO   Y. Hide-out that caught on fire

The Outsiders Matching 4 Answer Key

Q - 1.	GREASERS	A.	Pony is assigned to write one.
V - 2.	TURF	B.	Cherry is one for the Greasers.
D - 3.	RUMBLE	C.	Author
G - 4.	WINSTON	D.	Fight
E - 5.	BLOOD	E.	Red body fluid
X - 6.	KNIFE	F.	Darry hit Pony because he was ___.
P - 7.	PONYBOY	G.	Dally's last name
T - 8.	COKE	H.	Darry, Soda and Pony, for example
M - 9.	SMOKE	I.	Holden; He started a rumble
N - 10.	HAIRCUT	J.	Place were Johnny died
B - 11.	SPY	K.	Kind of sandwiches Johnny ate
K - 12.	BARBECUE	L.	Cherry's Soc sidekick
H - 13.	BROTHERS	M.	Firefighters get it; ____ inhalation
C - 14.	HINTON	N.	Getting one upset Pony because he lost his trademark.
Y - 15.	CHURCH	O.	Johnny killed him.
R - 16.	DOUBLE	P.	The narrator
A - 17.	THEME	Q.	East-end gang
J - 18.	HOSPITAL	R.	Nightly _____
W - 19.	OUTSIDERS	S.	He fought because everyone else did--to conform; ___-Bit
F - 20.	LATE	T.	Cherry threw hers into Dally's face.
L - 21.	MARCIA	U.	He killed Bob and saved the children.
U - 22.	JOHNNY	V.	Slang for area
O - 23.	BOB	W.	The _____; book title
I - 24.	PAUL	X.	Johnny's murder weapon
S - 25.	TWO	Y.	Hide-out that caught on fire

The Outsiders Magic Squares 1

Match the definition with the vocabulary word. Put your answers in the magic squares below. When your answers are correct, all columns and rows will add to the same number.

A. JUDGE   E. CIGARETTES   I. SOCS   M. ARM
B. KNIFE   F. BARBECUE   J. DARRY   N. OUTSIDERS
C. PAUL   G. FUN   K. RANDY   O. DOUBLE
D. TWO   H. TRAIN   L. LOT   P. FIGHT

1. Dally injured his getting Johnny out.
2. Kind of sandwiches Johnny ate
3. Transportation to Windrixville
4. Nightly _____
5. Pony and Johnny fell asleep in the empty _____.
6. Holden; He started a rumble
7. He acquitted Pony.
8. Pony's eldest brother
9. Tried to call off the big rumble
10. He fought because everyone else did--to conform; ____-Bit
11. Johnny's murder weapon
12. The West-end gang
13. The _____; book title
14. Pony smoked them
15. Soda fought for this reason.
16. Another name for rumble

A=	B=	C=	D=
E=	F=	G=	H=
I=	J=	K=	L=
M=	N=	O=	P=

The Outsiders Magic Squares 1 Answer Key

Match the definition with the vocabulary word. Put your answers in the magic squares below. When your answers are correct, all columns and rows will add to the same number.

A. JUDGE
B. KNIFE
C. PAUL
D. TWO
E. CIGARETTES
F. BARBECUE
G. FUN
H. TRAIN
I. SOCS
J. DARRY
K. RANDY
L. LOT
M. ARM
N. OUTSIDERS
O. DOUBLE
P. FIGHT

1. Dally injured his getting Johnny out.
2. Kind of sandwiches Johnny ate
3. Transportation to Windrixville
4. Nightly _____
5. Pony and Johnny fell asleep in the empty _____.
6. Holden; He started a rumble
7. He acquitted Pony.
8. Pony's eldest brother
9. Tried to call off the big rumble
10. He fought because everyone else did--to conform; ___-Bit
11. Johnny's murder weapon
12. The West-end gang
13. The _____; book title
14. Pony smoked them
15. Soda fought for this reason.
16. Another name for rumble

A=7	B=11	C=6	D=10
E=14	F=2	G=15	H=3
I=12	J=8	K=9	L=5
M=1	N=13	O=4	P=16

The Outsiders Magic Squares 2

Match the definition with the vocabulary word. Put your answers in the magic squares below. When your answers are correct, all columns and rows will add to the same number.

A. TWO   E. MOUNTAIN   I. DARRY   M. BOOK
B. BLOOD   F. HOSPITAL   J. GUN   N. SODAPOP
C. GALLANT   G. NEWSPAPER   K. LOT   O. SMOKE
D. BOB   H. JUDGE   L. BROTHERS   P. SPY

1. Red body fluid
2. Place for printed accounts of news
3. Pony and Johnny fell asleep in the empty _____.
4. Middle brother
5. Johnny's gift to Pony; Gone With the Wind
6. Darry, Soda and Pony, for example
7. He acquitted Pony.
8. He fought because everyone else did--to conform; ___-Bit
9. Cherry is one for the Greasers.
10. Pony's eldest brother
11. Jay's _____
12. Johnny killed him.
13. Johnny liked this land of southern gentlemen.
14. Place were Johnny died
15. Dally pointed an unloaded one at the police.
16. Firefighters get it; ____ inhalation

A=	B=	C=	D=
E=	F=	G=	H=
I=	J=	K=	L=
M=	N=	O=	P=

The Outsiders Magic Squares 2 Answer Key

Match the definition with the vocabulary word. Put your answers in the magic squares below. When your answers are correct, all columns and rows will add to the same number.

A. TWO   E. MOUNTAIN   I. DARRY   M. BOOK
B. BLOOD   F. HOSPITAL   J. GUN   N. SODAPOP
C. GALLANT   G. NEWSPAPER   K. LOT   O. SMOKE
D. BOB   H. JUDGE   L. BROTHERS   P. SPY

1. Red body fluid
2. Place for printed accounts of news
3. Pony and Johnny fell asleep in the empty _____.
4. Middle brother
5. Johnny's gift to Pony; Gone With the Wind
6. Darry, Soda and Pony, for example
7. He acquitted Pony.
8. He fought because everyone else did--to conform; ___-Bit
9. Cherry is one for the Greasers.
10. Pony's eldest brother
11. Jay's _____
12. Johnny killed him.
13. Johnny liked this land of southern gentlemen.
14. Place were Johnny died
15. Dally pointed an unloaded one at the police.
16. Firefighters get it; ____ inhalation

A=8	B=1	C=13	D=12
E=11	F=14	G=2	H=7
I=10	J=15	K=3	L=6
M=5	N=4	O=16	P=9

The Outsiders Magic Squares 3

Match the definition with the vocabulary word. Put your answers in the magic squares below. When your answers are correct, all columns and rows will add to the same number.

A. GOLDEN   E. RUMBLE   I. CHERRY   M. SPY
B. RANDY   F. CIGARETTES   J. BOOK   N. MOUNTAIN
C. GREASERS   G. OUTSIDERS   K. GOOD   O. PRIDE
D. BOTTLE   H. PONYBOY   L. FIGHT   P. ARM

1. Reason Darry fought; Pony's hair symbolized his
2. Pony broke the end off one and threatened Socs.
3. Johnny's gift to Pony; Gone With the Wind
4. Fight
5. She became a Greaser spy.
6. Pony smoked them
7. Dally injured his getting Johnny out.
8. East-end gang
9. The narrator
10. Johnny's note said that there is still _____ in the world.
11. What Johnny wanted Pony to stay
12. Jay's _____
13. Tried to call off the big rumble
14. Cherry is one for the Greasers.
15. The _____; book title
16. Another name for rumble

A=	B=	C=	D=
E=	F=	G=	H=
I=	J=	K=	L=
M=	N=	O=	P=

The Outsiders Magic Squares 3 Answer Key

Match the definition with the vocabulary word. Put your answers in the magic squares below. When your answers are correct, all columns and rows will add to the same number.

A. GOLDEN E. RUMBLE I. CHERRY M. SPY
B. RANDY F. CIGARETTES J. BOOK N. MOUNTAIN
C. GREASERS G. OUTSIDERS K. GOOD O. PRIDE
D. BOTTLE H. PONYBOY L. FIGHT P. ARM

1. Reason Darry fought; Pony's hair symbolized his
2. Pony broke the end off one and threatened Socs.
3. Johnny's gift to Pony; Gone With the Wind
4. Fight
5. She became a Greaser spy.
6. Pony smoked them
7. Dally injured his getting Johnny out.
8. East-end gang
9. The narrator
10. Johnny's note said that there is still _____ in the world.
11. What Johnny wanted Pony to stay
12. Jay's _____
13. Tried to call off the big rumble
14. Cherry is one for the Greasers.
15. The _____; book title
16. Another name for rumble

A=11	B=13	C=8	D=2
E=4	F=6	G=15	H=9
I=5	J=3	K=10	L=16
M=14	N=12	O=1	P=7

The Outsiders Magic Squares 4

Match the definition with the vocabulary word. Put your answers in the magic squares below. When your answers are correct, all columns and rows will add to the same number.

A. JOHNNY   E. TWO   I. BLUE   M. FIGHT
B. BLOOD   F. SMOKE   J. MUSTANG   N. SODAPOP
C. DARRY   G. GUN   K. DOUBLE   O. CHERRY
D. GREASERS   H. RINGS   L. GOOD   P. MOUNTAIN

1. Red body fluid
2. Dally pointed an unloaded one at the police.
3. Nightly _____
4. Middle brother
5. Another name for rumble
6. Johnny's note said that there is still _____ in the world.
7. Bob wore these on his fingers.
8. He killed Bob and saved the children.
9. Jay's _____
10. Mustang color
11. He fought because everyone else did--to conform; ___-Bit
12. East-end gang
13. Pony's eldest brother
14. Firefighters get it; ____ inhalation
15. Blue Soc car
16. She became a Greaser spy.

A=	B=	C=	D=
E=	F=	G=	H=
I=	J=	K=	L=
M=	N=	O=	P=

The Outsiders Magic Squares 4 Answer Key

Match the definition with the vocabulary word. Put your answers in the magic squares below. When your answers are correct, all columns and rows will add to the same number.

A. JOHNNY   E. TWO   I. BLUE   M. FIGHT
B. BLOOD   F. SMOKE   J. MUSTANG   N. SODAPOP
C. DARRY   G. GUN   K. DOUBLE   O. CHERRY
D. GREASERS   H. RINGS   L. GOOD   P. MOUNTAIN

1. Red body fluid
2. Dally pointed an unloaded one at the police.
3. Nightly _____
4. Middle brother
5. Another name for rumble
6. Johnny's note said that there is still _____ in the world.
7. Bob wore these on his fingers.
8. He killed Bob and saved the children.
9. Jay's _____
10. Mustang color
11. He fought because everyone else did--to conform; ____-Bit
12. East-end gang
13. Pony's eldest brother
14. Firefighters get it; ____ inhalation
15. Blue Soc car
16. She became a Greaser spy.

A=8	B=1	C=13	D=12
E=11	F=14	G=2	H=7
I=10	J=15	K=3	L=6
M=5	N=4	O=16	P=9

The Outsiders Word Search 1

Words are placed backwards, forward, diagonally, up and down. Clues listed below can help you find the words. Circle the hidden vocabulary words in the maze.

```
L R D N E W S P A P E R V T R A I N C
S M O K E H P H B D R G T H E M E J I
P A U L B C O S I L Y O T S T N E J G
T K B G F R J S B N A O O P U S R Y A
S E L B M U R S P Y T D M A R C I A R
O G E H D H N O B I A O E G F I F D E
R X U G H C N G F P T B N W B D D A T
F G E N F Y E K O C D A L L A S J E T
M I J D B O V P D L T R L X R G A D E
W R G O Q R U Z P S D B L H S N C T S
C E Y H H L M N U C H E R R Y I K I H
Q H N W T R M M T N J C N D B R E M T
B T N V A Z D B L A L U D K X L T Y P
Q O H B S D K L O A I E F I N K O M W
D M O S O C S U T W O N R A N D Y O F
T B J K F S R E D I S T U O Y R R A D
```

Another name for rumble (5)
Author (6)
Blue Soc car (7)
Bob wore these on his fingers. (5)
Cherry is one for the Greasers. (3)
Cherry threw hers into Dally's face. (4)
Cherry's Soc sidekick (6)
Condition of Bob, Dally and Johnny (4)
Dally injured his getting Johnny out. (3)
Dally pointed an unloaded one at the police. (3)
Darry hit Pony because he was ___. (4)
Fight (6)
Firefighters get it; ____ inhalation (5)
Gang symbol (6)
Hard-fighter Shepards first name (3)
He acquitted Pony. (5)
He fought because everyone else did--to conform; ___-Bit (3)
He killed Bob and saved the children. (6)
Hide-out that caught on fire (6)
Holden; He started a rumble (4)
Johnny killed him. (3)
Johnny rejected his _____'s visit. (6)
Johnny's gift to Pony; Gone With the Wind (4)
Johnny's murder weapon (5)
Johnny's note said that there is still _____ in the world. (4)
Kind of sandwiches Johnny ate (8)

Middle brother (7)
Mustang color (4)
Nightly _____ (6)
Place for printed accounts of news (9)
Place were Johnny died (8)
Poet Robert (5)
Police shot him (6)
Pony and Johnny fell asleep in the empty _____. (3)
Pony is assigned to write one. (5)
Pony smoked them (10)
Pony was almost drowned in it. (8)
Pony's eldest brother (5)
Reason Darry fought; Pony's hair symbolized his (5)
Red body fluid (5)
She became a Greaser spy. (6)
Slang for area (4)
Slang for knife (5)
Soda fought for this reason. (3)
The West-end gang (4)
The _____; book title (9)
The church caught on _____. (4)
The narrator (7)
Transportation to Windrixville (5)
Tried to call off the big rumble (5)
What Johnny wanted Pony to stay (6)

The Outsiders Word Search 1 Answer Key

Words are placed backwards, forward, diagonally, up and down. Clues listed below can help you find the words. Circle the hidden vocabulary words in the maze.

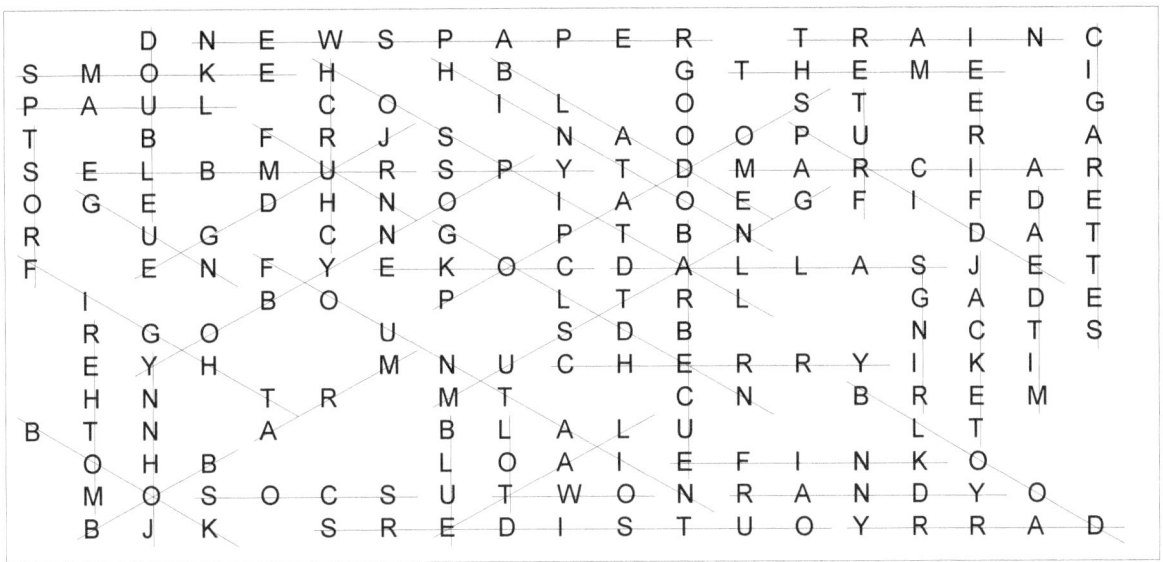

Another name for rumble (5)
Author (6)
Blue Soc car (7)
Bob wore these on his fingers. (5)
Cherry is one for the Greasers. (3)
Cherry threw hers into Dally's face. (4)
Cherry's Soc sidekick (6)
Condition of Bob, Dally and Johnny (4)
Dally injured his getting Johnny out. (3)
Dally pointed an unloaded one at the police. (3)
Darry hit Pony because he was ___. (4)
Fight (6)
Firefighters get it; ____ inhalation (5)
Gang symbol (6)
Hard-fighter Shepards first name (3)
He acquitted Pony. (5)
He fought because everyone else did--to conform; ___-Bit (3)
He killed Bob and saved the children. (6)
Hide-out that caught on fire (6)
Holden; He started a rumble (4)
Johnny killed him. (3)
Johnny rejected his _____'s visit. (6)
Johnny's gift to Pony; Gone With the Wind (4)
Johnny's murder weapon (5)
Johnny's note said that there is still _____ in the world. (4)
Kind of sandwiches Johnny ate (8)

Middle brother (7)
Mustang color (4)
Nightly _____ (6)
Place for printed accounts of news (9)
Place were Johnny died (8)
Poet Robert (5)
Police shot him (6)
Pony and Johnny fell asleep in the empty _____. (3)
Pony is assigned to write one. (5)
Pony smoked them (10)
Pony was almost drowned in it. (8)
Pony's eldest brother (5)
Reason Darry fought; Pony's hair symbolized his (5)
Red body fluid (5)
She became a Greaser spy. (6)
Slang for area (4)
Slang for knife (5)
Soda fought for this reason. (3)
The West-end gang (4)
The _____; book title (9)
The church caught on _____. (4)
The narrator (7)
Transportation to Windrixville (5)
Tried to call off the big rumble (5)
What Johnny wanted Pony to stay (6)

The Outsiders Word Search 2

Words are placed backwards, forward, diagonally, up and down. Clues listed below can help you find the words. Circle the hidden vocabulary words in the maze.

```
B R O T H E R S B O O K C O K E C Z J
H I N T O N Y Z F C S L W F I G H T W
D R S Z M O C K J S G N R T C T E H X
F H K K B U M F R X N V X D E U R T S
K U M Y A A S E X X I M A K L Q R P L
G U N F R O S T F I R E C B E E Y T Z
L O R C B A O O A A D A O K T N D R Z
P D I R E L H S C N J B O A N B N A B
S A P R C H W H Q S G M L H B E A I M
W P G T U R F E Y E S L O W T L R N V
P I L A E T L G L G D J J J U T A D V
B H N H L B H B T D A Q P A C T K D N
K L T S U L M E I U R L P R R O N O E
S O O O T U A J M J R P F Y I B I O P
M P D O R O R N Z E Y V Q M A D F G Q
T G O L D E N N T C H U R C H S E X Y
```

Another name for rumble (5)
Author (6)
Blue Soc car (7)
Bob wore these on his fingers. (5)
Cherry is one for the Greasers. (3)
Cherry threw hers into Dally's face. (4)
Cherry's Soc sidekick (6)
Condition of Bob, Dally and Johnny (4)
Dally injured his getting Johnny out. (3)
Dally pointed an unloaded one at the police. (3)
Dally's last name (7)
Darry hit Pony because he was ___. (4)
Darry, Soda and Pony, for example (8)
East-end gang (8)
Fight (6)
Firefighters get it; ____ inhalation (5)
Gang symbol (6)
Getting one upset Pony because he lost his trademark. (7)
Hard-fighter Shepards first name (3)
He acquitted Pony. (5)
He fought because everyone else did--to conform; ___-Bit (3)
He killed Bob and saved the children. (6)
Hide-out that caught on fire (6)
Holden; He started a rumble (4)
Johnny killed him. (3)
Johnny liked this land of southern gentlemen. (7)

Johnny rejected his _____'s visit. (6)
Johnny's gift to Pony; Gone With the Wind (4)
Johnny's murder weapon (5)
Johnny's note said that there is still _____ in the world. (4)
Kind of sandwiches Johnny ate (8)
Mustang color (4)
Nightly _____ (6)
Poet Robert (5)
Pony and Johnny fell asleep in the empty _____. (3)
Pony broke the end off one and threatened Socs. (6)
Pony is assigned to write one. (5)
Pony's eldest brother (5)
Reason Darry fought; Pony's hair symbolized his (5)
Red body fluid (5)
She became a Greaser spy. (6)
Slang for area (4)
Slang for knife (5)
Soda fought for this reason. (3)
The West-end gang (4)
The church caught on _____. (4)
The narrator (7)
Transportation to Windrixville (5)
Tried to call off the big rumble (5)
What Johnny wanted Pony to stay (6)

The Outsiders Word Search 2 Answer Key

Words are placed backwards, forward, diagonally, up and down. Clues listed below can help you find the words. Circle the hidden vocabulary words in the maze.

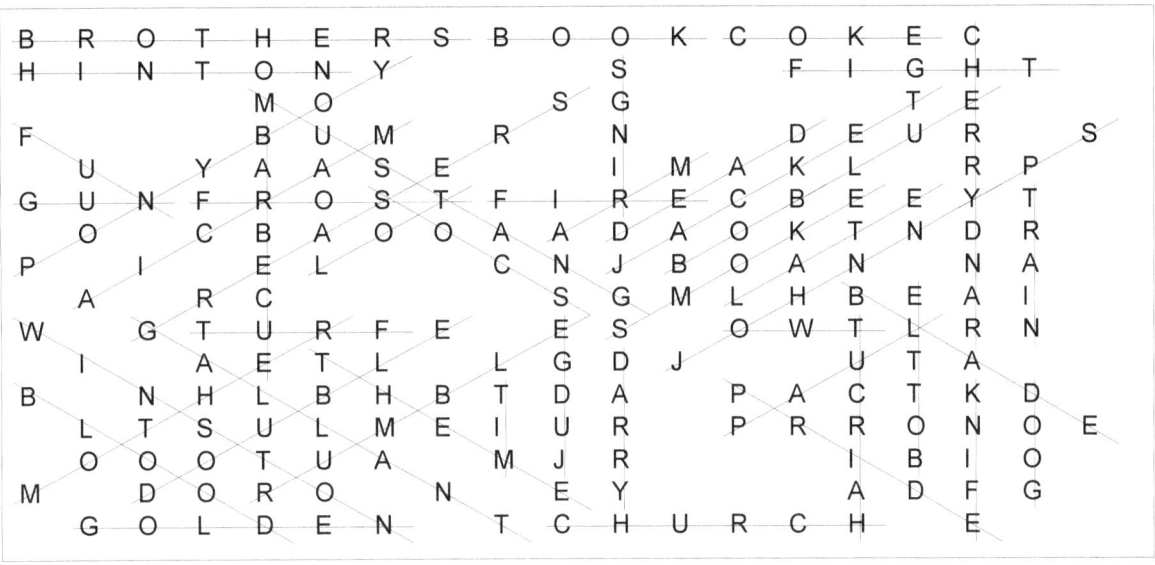

Another name for rumble (5)
Author (6)
Blue Soc car (7)
Bob wore these on his fingers. (5)
Cherry is one for the Greasers. (3)
Cherry threw hers into Dally's face. (4)
Cherry's Soc sidekick (6)
Condition of Bob, Dally and Johnny (4)
Dally injured his getting Johnny out. (3)
Dally pointed an unloaded one at the police. (3)
Dally's last name (7)
Darry hit Pony because he was ___. (4)
Darry, Soda and Pony, for example (8)
East-end gang (8)
Fight (6)
Firefighters get it; ____ inhalation (5)
Gang symbol (6)
Getting one upset Pony because he lost his trademark. (7)
Hard-fighter Shepards first name (3)
He acquitted Pony. (5)
He fought because everyone else did--to conform; ___-Bit (3)
He killed Bob and saved the children. (6)
Hide-out that caught on fire (6)
Holden; He started a rumble (4)
Johnny killed him. (3)
Johnny liked this land of southern gentlemen. (7)

Johnny rejected his _____'s visit. (6)
Johnny's gift to Pony; Gone With the Wind (4)
Johnny's murder weapon (5)
Johnny's note said that there is still _____ in the world. (4)
Kind of sandwiches Johnny ate (8)
Mustang color (4)
Nightly _____ (6)
Poet Robert (5)
Pony and Johnny fell asleep in the empty _____. (3)
Pony broke the end off one and threatened Socs. (6)
Pony is assigned to write one. (5)
Pony's eldest brother (5)
Reason Darry fought; Pony's hair symbolized his (5)
Red body fluid (5)
She became a Greaser spy. (6)
Slang for area (4)
Slang for knife (5)
Soda fought for this reason. (3)
The West-end gang (4)
The church caught on _____. (4)
The narrator (7)
Transportation to Windrixville (5)
Tried to call off the big rumble (5)
What Johnny wanted Pony to stay (6)

The Outsiders Word Search 3

Words are placed backwards, forward, diagonally, up and down. Words listed below are included in the maze. Circle the hidden vocabulary words in the maze.

```
B L U E B G P G C I G A R E T T E S D N
O A J G M O N U O B D O F H J U U A A X
U T M R W O T N K L G I L S Q R C L R X
T I A R I D R T E P N G G D P F E L R X
S P R E N D I B L K A T A R E Y B A Y R
I S C P S Z N V B E T U L M D N R D G Q
D O I A T S G X M M S S L S R V A T G L
E H A P O L S N U N U R A Y Q Y B V M P
R H T S N D I Y R Q M E N H N R B Y K S
S B I W M A Q J T G Y H T N V W A Y J M
S O M E T N T T O Z B T H W M P L N U T
N O T N I H T E L B U O D W O P R I D E
R K U A G U K K S S J R B P T Z P A G Y
G O R D C O F C L J B B A F H B E L E D
M T F R M C I A D G L D F Z E D L T B F
F W I S Z Z R J H Q O C H U R C H A T L
L A G H Q N E S R S O M C J N E C S D J
H C H E R R Y J R F D D Z N M X O D C E
L A T E F O U N T A I N T E P R F T C N
S O C S R E S A E R G K K S F G T C C Q
```

ARM	COKE	GOOD	MARCIA	SOCS
BARBECUE	DALLAS	GREASERS	MOTHER	SODAPOP
BLADE	DARRY	GUN	MOUNTAIN	SPY
BLOOD	DEAD	HAIRCUT	MUSTANG	THEME
BLUE	DOUBLE	HINTON	NEWSPAPER	TIM
BOB	FIGHT	HOSPITAL	OUTSIDERS	TRAIN
BOOK	FIRE	JACKET	PAUL	TURF
BOTTLE	FOUNTAIN	JOHNNY	PRIDE	TWO
BROTHERS	FROST	JUDGE	RANDY	WINSTON
CHERRY	FUN	KNIFE	RINGS	
CHURCH	GALLANT	LATE	RUMBLE	
CIGARETTES	GOLDEN	LOT	SMOKE	

The Outsiders Word Search 3 Answer Key

Words are placed backwards, forward, diagonally, up and down. Words listed below are included in the maze. Circle the hidden vocabulary words in the maze.

```
B  L  U  E  B  G     G  C  I  G  A  R  E  T  T  E  S  D
O  A        M  O     U  O        O  F        U  U  A  A
U  T  M  R  W  O  T  N  K     G  I  L  S     R  C  L  R
T  I  A  R  I  D  R  T  E  P     N  G  D  P  F  E  L  R
S  P  R  E  N     I     L  K  A     A     E  Y  B  A  Y
I     S  C  P     N     B  E  T  U  L        N  R  D
D     O  I  A  T     G     M     S  S  L        A
E     H  A  P  O     S  N  U     U  R  A     Y  B
R        T  S  N        I     R     M  E  N     R
S  B     I  W        A        T        H  T  N     A     J
   O  M  E        T     T  O     B  T  H  W  M  P     N  U
N  O  T  N  I  H  T  E  L  B  U  O  D        O  P  R  I  D  E
   K  U  A        U  K  K        J  R  B  P  T        A  G  Y
   O  R        C  O  F  C        B  B  A     H  B  E     E
M  T  F  R  M     I  A        L  D  F     E  D  L  T
      I     S        R  J        O  C  H  U  R  C  H  A  T
   A  G              E        S  O              N  E     S  D
H  C  H  E  R  R  Y           D              M        O     E
L  A  T  E  F  O  U  N  T  A  I  N        E        R
S  O  C  S  R  E  S  A  E  R  G                 F
```

ARM	COKE	GOOD	MARCIA	SOCS
BARBECUE	DALLAS	GREASERS	MOTHER	SODAPOP
BLADE	DARRY	GUN	MOUNTAIN	SPY
BLOOD	DEAD	HAIRCUT	MUSTANG	THEME
BLUE	DOUBLE	HINTON	NEWSPAPER	TIM
BOB	FIGHT	HOSPITAL	OUTSIDERS	TRAIN
BOOK	FIRE	JACKET	PAUL	TURF
BOTTLE	FOUNTAIN	JOHNNY	PRIDE	TWO
BROTHERS	FROST	JUDGE	RANDY	WINSTON
CHERRY	FUN	KNIFE	RINGS	
CHURCH	GALLANT	LATE	RUMBLE	
CIGARETTES	GOLDEN	LOT	SMOKE	

The Outsiders Word Search 4

Words are placed backwards, forward, diagonally, up and down. Words listed below are included in the maze. Circle the hidden vocabulary words in the maze.

```
S Z J S H W L D F P M U S T A N G Y H W
Z O U R T I Q Q L O B A R B E C U E Q W
M N D V B N W K N N T Q F W H S E S V F
Z Y G A C S Q F X Y T V I M X S D D D N
Z V E Y P T B D R B C F R N B P I P E J
G B F B O O K B R O T H E R S Y R R A D
P C M S B N P L U Y S L H C J E P C D Y
R O K T F N A T S N B T O W H H K K N S
J K D N K T S C S M Q S H T C E H P E C
J E Z J I I W T U R F D O G T I M S W Z
L R G P D F N R D D O M H O N W N G S T
D D S E F A E S H O K H L P I T O N P J
D O R H L I H E L T T O B M A R C I A W
H S U L D F G B B R G G L G T H H R P J
B K A B A Z U H R Y J O U O N A E T E M
L G Y J L H I N T O N O E L U I R R Z
A D T W L E Z Z H H L D U D O R R A P
D W F S A P G N P B E A R E F C Y I N J
E K O M S K N F B P P M T N G U N N D F
K F D D H Y C H U R C H E E F T Q R Y X
```

ARM	COKE	GOLDEN	LOT	RUMBLE
BARBECUE	DALLAS	GOOD	MARCIA	SMOKE
BLADE	DARRY	GUN	MOTHER	SOCS
BLOOD	DEAD	HAIRCUT	MUSTANG	SODAPOP
BLUE	DOUBLE	HINTON	NEWSPAPER	SPY
BOB	FIGHT	HOSPITAL	OUTSIDERS	THEME
BOOK	FIRE	JACKET	PAUL	TIM
BOTTLE	FOUNTAIN	JOHNNY	PONYBOY	TRAIN
BROTHERS	FROST	JUDGE	PRIDE	TURF
CHERRY	FUN	KNIFE	RANDY	TWO
CHURCH	GALLANT	LATE	RINGS	WINSTON

The Outsiders Word Search 4 Answer Key

Words are placed backwards, forward, diagonally, up and down. Words listed below are included in the maze. Circle the hidden vocabulary words in the maze.

ARM	COKE	GOLDEN	LOT	RUMBLE
BARBECUE	DALLAS	GOOD	MARCIA	SMOKE
BLADE	DARRY	GUN	MOTHER	SOCS
BLOOD	DEAD	HAIRCUT	MUSTANG	SODAPOP
BLUE	DOUBLE	HINTON	NEWSPAPER	SPY
BOB	FIGHT	HOSPITAL	OUTSIDERS	THEME
BOOK	FIRE	JACKET	PAUL	TIM
BOTTLE	FOUNTAIN	JOHNNY	PONYBOY	TRAIN
BROTHERS	FROST	JUDGE	PRIDE	TURF
CHERRY	FUN	KNIFE	RANDY	TWO
CHURCH	GALLANT	LATE	RINGS	WINSTON

The Outsiders Crossword 1

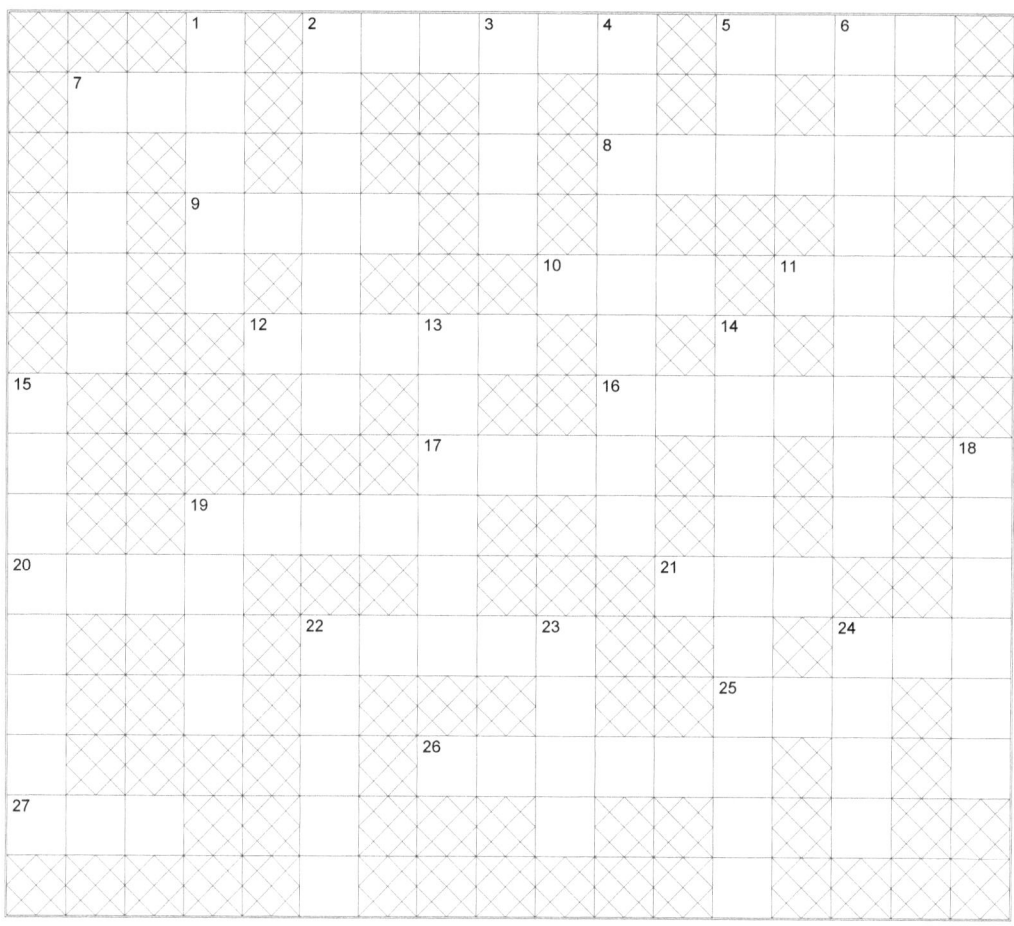

Across
2. Author
5. Johnny's note said that there is still _____ in the world.
7. Soda fought for this reason.
8. Dally's last name
9. The church caught on _____.
10. Cherry is one for the Greasers.
11. Hard-fighter Shepards first name
12. He acquitted Pony.
16. Reason Darry fought; Pony's hair symbolized his
17. Darry hit Pony because he was ___.
19. Red body fluid
20. Holden; He started a rumble
21. Dally injured his getting Johnny out.
22. Bob wore these on his fingers.
24. Johnny killed him.
25. He fought because everyone else did--to conform; ___-Bit
26. Gang symbol
27. Pony and Johnny fell asleep in the empty _____.

Down
1. Johnny's murder weapon
2. Getting one upset Pony because he lost his trademark.
3. Slang for area
4. Place for printed accounts of news
5. Dally pointed an unloaded one at the police.
6. The _____; book title
7. Poet Robert
13. What Johnny wanted Pony to stay
14. Pony smoked them
15. Place were Johnny died
18. Fight
19. Mustang color
22. Tried to call off the big rumble
23. The West-end gang
24. Johnny's gift to Pony; Gone With the Wind

The Outsiders Crossword 1 Answer Key

		1 K	2 H	I	3 N	T	4 O	N		5 G	6 O	O	D	
	7 F	U	N		A		U		E		U		U	
		R		I		I		R		8 W	I	N	S	T	O	N
		O		9 F	I	R	E		F		S			S	
		S		E		C				10 S	P	Y	11 T	I	M
		T			12 J	U	D	13 G	E		A		14 C		D
15 H						T		O			16 P	R	I	D	E
O								17 L	A	T	E		G		R	18 R
S			19 B	L	O	O	D				R		A		S	U
20 P	A	U	L			E				21 A	R	M			M
I			U	22 R	I	N	G	23 S			E		24 B	O	B
T			E		A			O			25 T	W	O		L
A					26 J	A	C	K	E	T		O		E
27 L	O	T		D				S			E		K	
				Y						S				

Across
2. Author
5. Johnny's note said that there is still _____ in the world.
7. Soda fought for this reason.
8. Dally's last name
9. The church caught on _____.
10. Cherry is one for the Greasers.
11. Hard-fighter Shepards first name
12. He acquitted Pony.
16. Reason Darry fought; Pony's hair symbolized his
17. Darry hit Pony because he was ___.
19. Red body fluid
20. Holden; He started a rumble
21. Dally injured his getting Johnny out.
22. Bob wore these on his fingers.
24. Johnny killed him.
25. He fought because everyone else did--to conform; ___-Bit
26. Gang symbol
27. Pony and Johnny fell asleep in the empty _____.

Down
1. Johnny's murder weapon
2. Getting one upset Pony because he lost his trademark.
3. Slang for area
4. Place for printed accounts of news
5. Dally pointed an unloaded one at the police.
6. The _____; book title
7. Poet Robert
13. What Johnny wanted Pony to stay
14. Pony smoked them
15. Place were Johnny died
18. Fight
19. Mustang color
22. Tried to call off the big rumble
23. The West-end gang
24. Johnny's gift to Pony; Gone With the Wind

The Outsiders Crossword 2

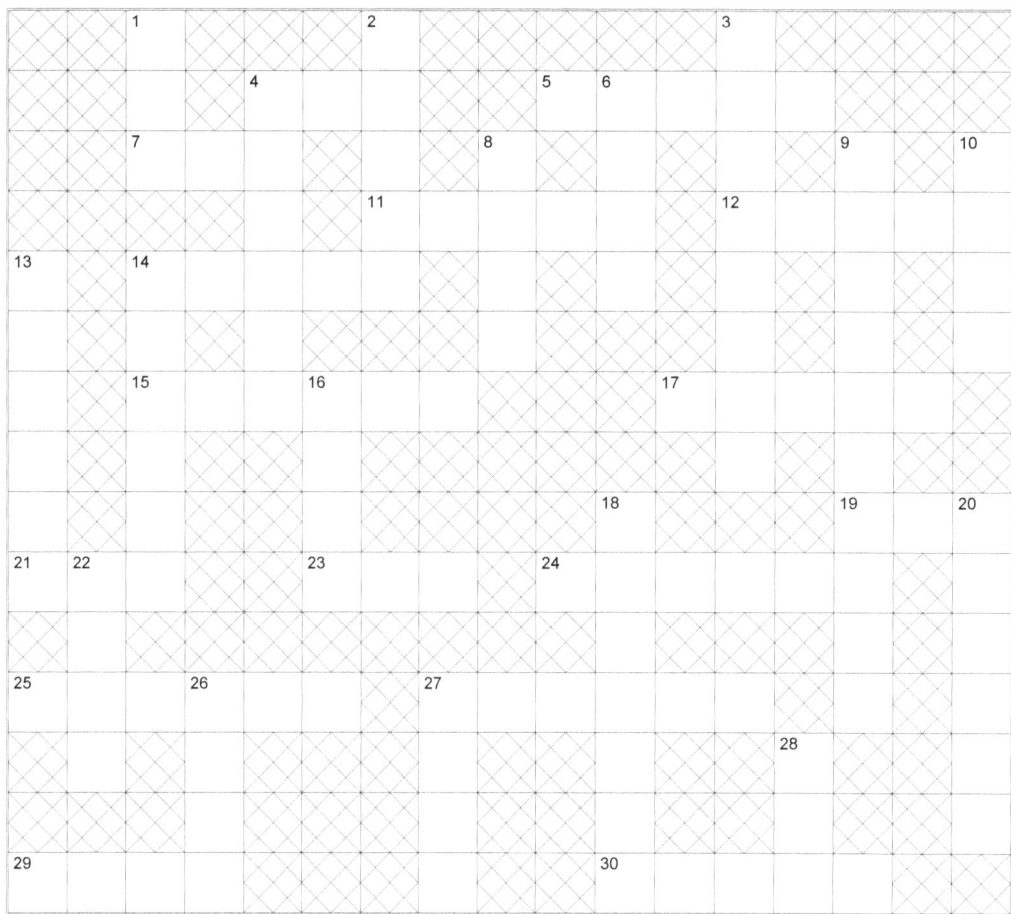

Across
4. Dally pointed an unloaded one at the police.
5. Red body fluid
7. He fought because everyone else did--to conform; ___-Bit
11. Poet Robert
12. Reason Darry fought; Pony's hair symbolized his
14. He acquitted Pony.
15. Author
17. Pony's eldest brother
19. Hard-fighter Shepards first name
21. Cherry is one for the Greasers.
23. Soda fought for this reason.
24. Gang symbol
25. Fight
27. Hide-out that caught on fire
29. The church caught on _____.
30. Pony is assigned to write one.

Down
1. Pony and Johnny fell asleep in the empty _____.
2. Johnny's murder weapon
3. Place were Johnny died
4. What Johnny wanted Pony to stay
6. Darry hit Pony because he was ___.
8. The West-end gang
9. Pony smoked them
10. Condition of Bob, Dally and Johnny
13. Police shot him
14. He killed Bob and saved the children.
16. Slang for area
18. Getting one upset Pony because he lost his trademark.
20. Cherry's Soc sidekick
22. Holden; He started a rumble
26. Mustang color
27. Cherry threw hers into Dally's face.
28. Dally injured his getting Johnny out.

The Outsiders Crossword 2 Answer Key

	1 L		2 K			3 H		
	O	4 G	U	N	5 B	6 L	O	O	D
	7 T	W	O		8 I	S	A	S	9 C	10 D
		L	11 F	R	O	S	T	12 P	R	I	D	E
13 D	14 J	U	D	G	E		C		E		I		G		A
A	O		E				S				T		A		D
L	15 H	I	16 N	T	O	N			17 D	A	R	R	Y
L		N		U						L		E
A		N		R				18 H			19 T	I	20 M
21 S	22 P	Y		23 F	U	N	24 J	A	C	K	E	T	A
	A						I				E	R
25 R	U	26 M	B	L	E	27 C	H	U	R	C	H		S		C
	L		L			O			C		28 A			I
	U		U			K			U		R			A
29 F	I	R	E			E		30 T	H	E	M	E

Across
4. Dally pointed an unloaded one at the police.
5. Red body fluid
7. He fought because everyone else did--to conform; ___-Bit
11. Poet Robert
12. Reason Darry fought; Pony's hair symbolized his
14. He acquitted Pony.
15. Author
17. Pony's eldest brother
19. Hard-fighter Shepards first name
21. Cherry is one for the Greasers.
23. Soda fought for this reason.
24. Gang symbol
25. Fight
27. Hide-out that caught on fire
29. The church caught on _____.
30. Pony is assigned to write one.

Down
1. Pony and Johnny fell asleep in the empty _____.
2. Johnny's murder weapon
3. Place were Johnny died
4. What Johnny wanted Pony to stay
6. Darry hit Pony because he was ___.
8. The West-end gang
9. Pony smoked them
10. Condition of Bob, Dally and Johnny
13. Police shot him
14. He killed Bob and saved the children.
16. Slang for area
18. Getting one upset Pony because he lost his trademark.
20. Cherry's Soc sidekick
22. Holden; He started a rumble
26. Mustang color
27. Cherry threw hers into Dally's face.
28. Dally injured his getting Johnny out.

The Outsiders Crossword 3

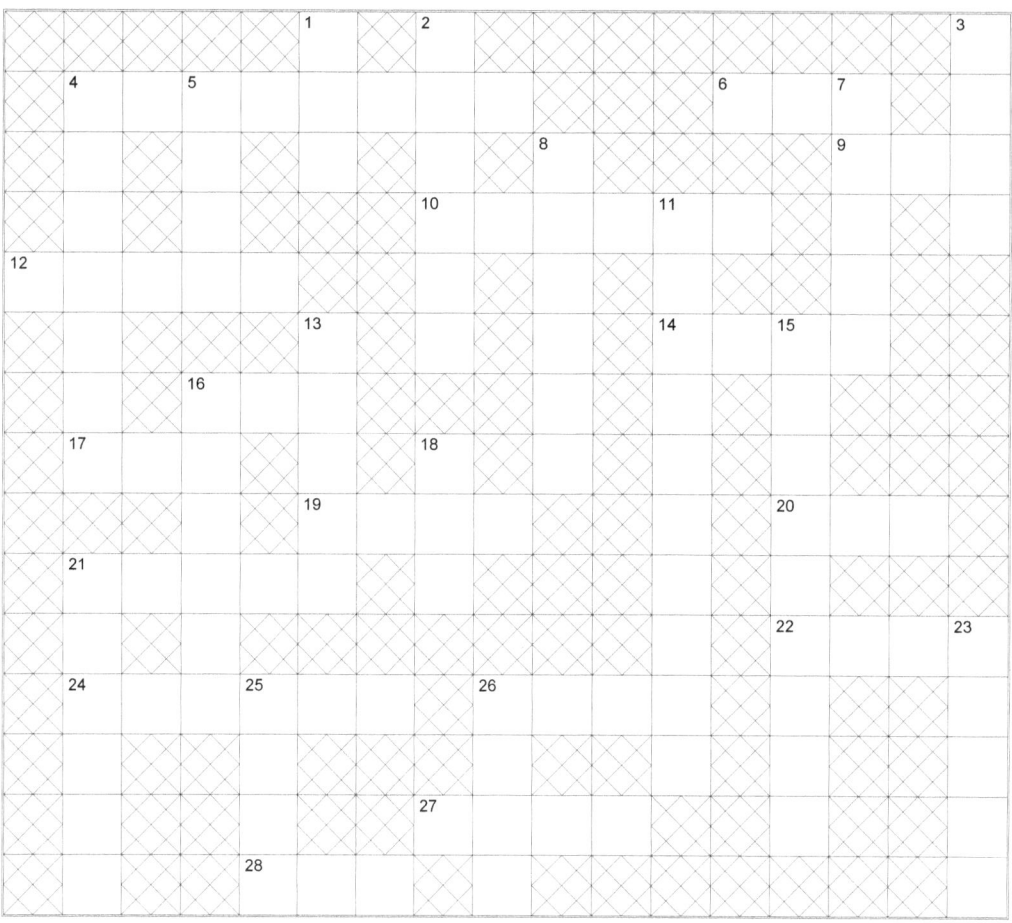

Across
4. Place were Johnny died
6. Johnny killed him.
9. Pony and Johnny fell asleep in the empty _____.
10. Hide-out that caught on fire
12. Poet Robert
14. Johnny's note said that there is still _____ in the world.
16. Dally pointed an unloaded one at the police.
17. He fought because everyone else did--to conform; ___-Bit
19. The church caught on _____.
20. Cherry is one for the Greasers.
21. He acquitted Pony.
22. Condition of Bob, Dally and Johnny
24. Author
26. Mustang color
27. Cherry threw hers into Dally's face.
28. Soda fought for this reason.

Down
1. Hard-fighter Shepards first name
2. Cherry's Soc sidekick
3. Darry hit Pony because he was ___.
4. Getting one upset Pony because he lost his trademark.
5. The West-end gang
7. Red body fluid
8. Fight
11. Pony smoked them
13. Johnny's murder weapon
15. The _____; book title
16. What Johnny wanted Pony to stay
18. Dally injured his getting Johnny out.
21. He killed Bob and saved the children.
23. Pony's eldest brother
25. Slang for area
26. Johnny's gift to Pony; Gone With the Wind

The Outsiders Crossword 3 Answer Key

					1 T	2 M					6	7		3 L
	4 H	O	5 S	P	I	T	A	L			B	O	B	A
	A		O		M		R		8 R			9 L	O	T
	I		C			10 C	H	U	R	11 C	H	O		E
12 F	R	O	S	T		I			M		I		O	
	C			13 K	A		B		14 G	15 O	O	D		
	U	16 G	U	N			L		A		U			
17 T	W	O		I	18 A		E		R		T			
		L		19 F	I	R	E		E		20 S	P	Y	
21 J	U	D	G	E		M			T		I			
O		E							T		22 D	E	A	23 D
24 H	I	N	25 T	O	N		26 B	L	U	E	E			A
N			U				O			S		R		R
N			R			27 C	O	K	E			S		R
Y			28 F	U	N		K							Y

Across
4. Place were Johnny died
6. Johnny killed him.
9. Pony and Johnny fell asleep in the empty _____.
10. Hide-out that caught on fire
12. Poet Robert
14. Johnny's note said that there is still _____ in the world.
16. Dally pointed an unloaded one at the police.
17. He fought because everyone else did--to conform; ___-Bit
19. The church caught on _____.
20. Cherry is one for the Greasers.
21. He acquitted Pony.
22. Condition of Bob, Dally and Johnny
24. Author
26. Mustang color
27. Cherry threw hers into Dally's face.
28. Soda fought for this reason.

Down
1. Hard-fighter Shepards first name
2. Cherry's Soc sidekick
3. Darry hit Pony because he was ___.
4. Getting one upset Pony because he lost his trademark.
5. The West-end gang
7. Red body fluid
8. Fight
11. Pony smoked them
13. Johnny's murder weapon
15. The _____; book title
16. What Johnny wanted Pony to stay
18. Dally injured his getting Johnny out.
21. He killed Bob and saved the children.
23. Pony's eldest brother
25. Slang for area
26. Johnny's gift to Pony; Gone With the Wind

The Outsiders Crossword 4

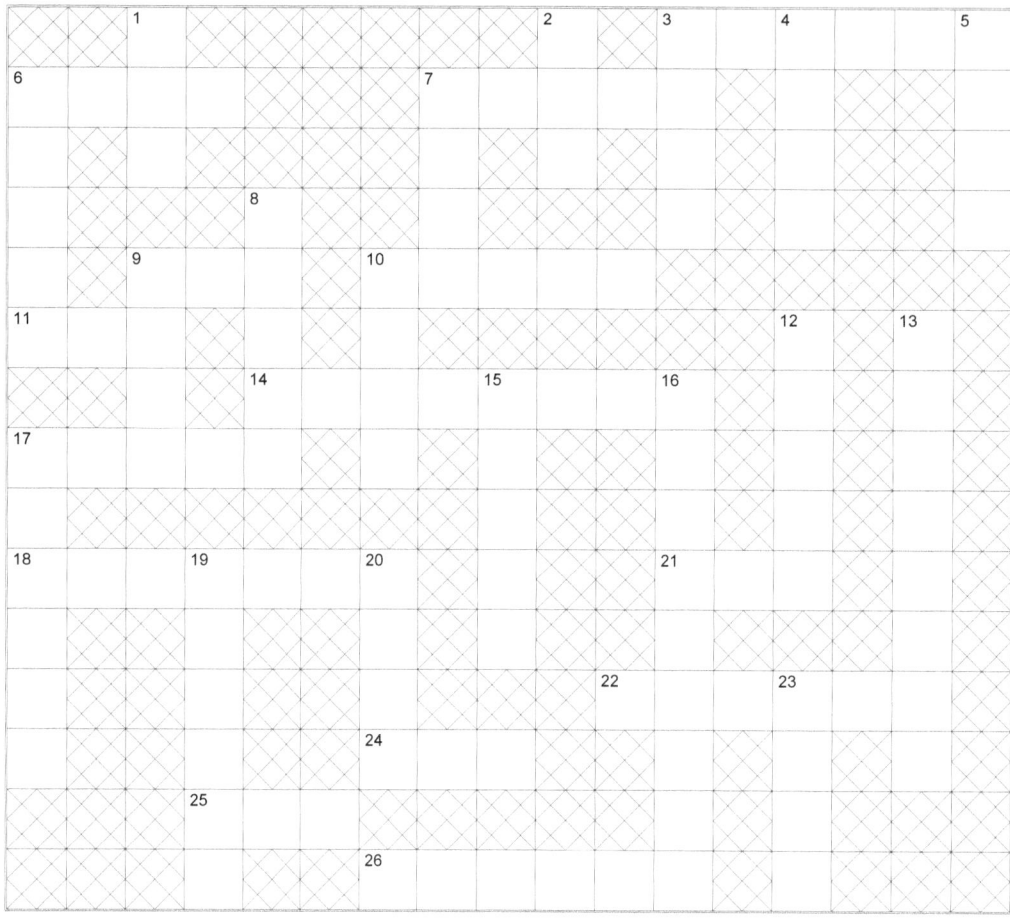

Across
3. Police shot him
6. The church caught on _____.
7. Reason Darry fought; Pony's hair symbolized his
9. Dally pointed an unloaded one at the police.
10. Red body fluid
11. He fought because everyone else did--to conform; ___-Bit
14. Pony was almost drowned in it.
17. He acquitted Pony.
18. Getting one upset Pony because he lost his trademark.
21. Cherry is one for the Greasers.
22. Cherry's Soc sidekick
24. Soda fought for this reason.
25. Pony and Johnny fell asleep in the empty _____.
26. Johnny rejected his _____'s visit.

Down
1. Dally injured his getting Johnny out.
2. Hard-fighter Shepards first name
3. Condition of Bob, Dally and Johnny
4. Darry hit Pony because he was ___.
5. The West-end gang
6. Poet Robert
7. Holden; He started a rumble
8. Johnny's murder weapon
9. Johnny's note said that there is still _____ in the world.
10. Mustang color
12. Pony's eldest brother
13. Place were Johnny died
15. Pony is assigned to write one.
16. Place for printed accounts of news
17. He killed Bob and saved the children.
19. Fight
20. Slang for area
23. Cherry threw hers into Dally's face.

The Outsiders Crossword 4 Answer Key

	1				2	3		4		5
	A				T	D	A	L	L	A	S
6 F	I	R	E		7 P	R	I	D	E	A		O
R	M				A		M	A		T		C
O		8 K			U			D		E		S
S	9 G	U	N		10 B	L	O	O	D			
11 T	W	O		I		L				12 D	13 H
		O		14 F	O	U	N	15 T	A	16 I	N	A	O
17 J	U	D	G	E		E		H		E		R	S
O						E				W		R	P
18 H	A	19 I	R	C	U	20 T		M		21 S	P	Y	I
N		U				U		E		P			T
N		M				R		22 M	A	23 R	C	I	A
Y		B				24 F	U	N		P		O	L
		25 L	O	T						E		K	
		E				26 M	O	T	H	E	R	E	

Across
- 3. Police shot him
- 6. The church caught on _____.
- 7. Reason Darry fought; Pony's hair symbolized his
- 9. Dally pointed an unloaded one at the police.
- 10. Red body fluid
- 11. He fought because everyone else did--to conform; ___-Bit
- 14. Pony was almost drowned in it.
- 17. He acquitted Pony.
- 18. Getting one upset Pony because he lost his trademark.
- 21. Cherry is one for the Greasers.
- 22. Cherry's Soc sidekick
- 24. Soda fought for this reason.
- 25. Pony and Johnny fell asleep in the empty _____.
- 26. Johnny rejected his _____'s visit.

Down
- 1. Dally injured his getting Johnny out.
- 2. Hard-fighter Shepards first name
- 3. Condition of Bob, Dally and Johnny
- 4. Darry hit Pony because he was ___.
- 5. The West-end gang
- 6. Poet Robert
- 7. Holden; He started a rumble
- 8. Johnny's murder weapon
- 9. Johnny's note said that there is still _____ in the world.
- 10. Mustang color
- 12. Pony's eldest brother
- 13. Place were Johnny died
- 15. Pony is assigned to write one.
- 16. Place for printed accounts of news
- 17. He killed Bob and saved the children.
- 19. Fight
- 20. Slang for area
- 23. Cherry threw hers into Dally's face.

The Outsiders

BARBECUE	DEAD	MUSTANG	NEWSPAPER	RUMBLE
SODAPOP	GOOD	MOTHER	GALLANT	HINTON
SMOKE	SOCS	FREE SPACE	OUTSIDERS	PRIDE
FOUNTAIN	DALLAS	FROST	JOHNNY	RINGS
BOTTLE	TWO	BROTHERS	CHERRY	BOB

The Outsiders

THEME	RANDY	GUN	JACKET	TURF
HAIRCUT	ARM	LATE	LOT	DARRY
TIM	FUN	FREE SPACE	FIGHT	JUDGE
CIGARETTES	GREASERS	TRAIN	PONYBOY	HOSPITAL
BLOOD	COKE	GOLDEN	DOUBLE	BLADE

The Outsiders

JACKET	SOCS	BARBECUE	BLADE	JUDGE
DOUBLE	OUTSIDERS	KNIFE	FUN	BROTHERS
RANDY	SODAPOP	FREE SPACE	TWO	TIM
SPY	CHURCH	PONYBOY	ARM	FROST
HINTON	PRIDE	GREASERS	BLUE	BOOK

The Outsiders

MOUNTAIN	LATE	CHERRY	TRAIN	CIGARETTES
RUMBLE	BOB	GOLDEN	FIRE	RINGS
LOT	THEME	FREE SPACE	JOHNNY	GUN
TURF	DEAD	PAUL	SMOKE	DARRY
NEWSPAPER	BLOOD	GOOD	HOSPITAL	COKE

The Outsiders

ARM	SODAPOP	JACKET	TRAIN	MOTHER
TIM	BOOK	MOUNTAIN	RANDY	CIGARETTES
COKE	CHURCH	FREE SPACE	FOUNTAIN	FUN
THEME	OUTSIDERS	DEAD	MUSTANG	JUDGE
LATE	GUN	RUMBLE	GALLANT	GOLDEN

The Outsiders

TURF	FIGHT	SPY	GREASERS	TWO
KNIFE	NEWSPAPER	GOOD	BARBECUE	HINTON
FROST	BOB	FREE SPACE	BROTHERS	PONYBOY
JOHNNY	HOSPITAL	PRIDE	BOTTLE	MARCIA
DOUBLE	CHERRY	SMOKE	HAIRCUT	RINGS

The Outsiders

RANDY	THEME	TRAIN	HINTON	MOUNTAIN
FOUNTAIN	GOLDEN	PONYBOY	HAIRCUT	JUDGE
DARRY	GREASERS	FREE SPACE	BOTTLE	JOHNNY
TIM	CHURCH	FROST	FIGHT	HOSPITAL
LATE	SODAPOP	GALLANT	RINGS	SMOKE

The Outsiders

NEWSPAPER	LOT	PRIDE	ARM	TWO
SPY	BOB	FUN	COKE	FIRE
DALLAS	TURF	FREE SPACE	BLADE	MOTHER
MUSTANG	MARCIA	GUN	CHERRY	OUTSIDERS
BOOK	BLUE	GOOD	DOUBLE	BLOOD

The Outsiders

MARCIA	BARBECUE	GOLDEN	CHURCH	DALLAS
SODAPOP	COKE	BLUE	KNIFE	BOOK
WINSTON	HOSPITAL	FREE SPACE	MOUNTAIN	PRIDE
JUDGE	PAUL	GREASERS	RINGS	FIRE
THEME	MOTHER	FUN	FOUNTAIN	BOB

The Outsiders

CHERRY	SPY	JOHNNY	GOOD	LOT
MUSTANG	PONYBOY	OUTSIDERS	ARM	HAIRCUT
DOUBLE	LATE	FREE SPACE	GALLANT	NEWSPAPER
DARRY	CIGARETTES	TIM	GUN	BROTHERS
BLOOD	JACKET	DEAD	FROST	BLADE

The Outsiders

OUTSIDERS	MOUNTAIN	GREASERS	DEAD	CHURCH
MARCIA	GOOD	FIRE	GOLDEN	DOUBLE
JUDGE	CHERRY	FREE SPACE	BOB	SODAPOP
TIM	GUN	TURF	THEME	KNIFE
FROST	JOHNNY	ARM	HOSPITAL	PAUL

The Outsiders

FIGHT	PRIDE	NEWSPAPER	SPY	PONYBOY
BLADE	HINTON	FUN	GALLANT	MOTHER
RANDY	TWO	FREE SPACE	LOT	DARRY
BOOK	HAIRCUT	RUMBLE	WINSTON	RINGS
SOCS	FOUNTAIN	JACKET	BLUE	LATE

The Outsiders

NEWSPAPER	BARBECUE	PONYBOY	GUN	HAIRCUT
BOTTLE	SPY	CIGARETTES	PAUL	FUN
FIGHT	KNIFE	FREE SPACE	SOCS	GOOD
GREASERS	JOHNNY	LOT	BOB	MOTHER
BLOOD	BROTHERS	GALLANT	CHERRY	SMOKE

The Outsiders

HINTON	MARCIA	GOLDEN	LATE	RINGS
BLADE	TRAIN	OUTSIDERS	CHURCH	TWO
SODAPOP	FOUNTAIN	FREE SPACE	COKE	HOSPITAL
BLUE	ARM	THEME	DALLAS	RUMBLE
DARRY	MOUNTAIN	FROST	TURF	FIRE

The Outsiders

SMOKE	BLUE	GREASERS	BOOK	LATE
BOB	HINTON	MARCIA	BROTHERS	HOSPITAL
GOOD	FIGHT	FREE SPACE	BLOOD	MUSTANG
CHERRY	MOTHER	RUMBLE	GUN	JOHNNY
CHURCH	TURF	FUN	COKE	CIGARETTES

The Outsiders

JUDGE	PRIDE	RANDY	OUTSIDERS	THEME
GOLDEN	FROST	HAIRCUT	SODAPOP	BOTTLE
PONYBOY	NEWSPAPER	FREE SPACE	DOUBLE	JACKET
DALLAS	ARM	WINSTON	KNIFE	TRAIN
SPY	DEAD	BARBECUE	FIRE	BLADE

The Outsiders

SODAPOP	FOUNTAIN	MOUNTAIN	BARBECUE	BOOK
GUN	PAUL	JOHNNY	OUTSIDERS	PONYBOY
SMOKE	MUSTANG	FREE SPACE	LATE	FIGHT
RINGS	JACKET	SPY	CHURCH	HOSPITAL
DALLAS	JUDGE	CIGARETTES	FIRE	SOCS

The Outsiders

WINSTON	GALLANT	TRAIN	PRIDE	NEWSPAPER
BOTTLE	RUMBLE	FUN	CHERRY	MOTHER
GREASERS	COKE	FREE SPACE	BOB	KNIFE
TURF	THEME	MARCIA	BLUE	HINTON
TWO	DARRY	FROST	TIM	DEAD

The Outsiders

MOUNTAIN	FOUNTAIN	RANDY	BLOOD	BOB
SOCS	BROTHERS	WINSTON	DALLAS	DARRY
FROST	GOLDEN	FREE SPACE	PAUL	SMOKE
GREASERS	HINTON	MARCIA	CIGARETTES	TWO
LOT	COKE	TIM	DEAD	NEWSPAPER

The Outsiders

LATE	TRAIN	HOSPITAL	RUMBLE	TURF
MOTHER	OUTSIDERS	ARM	BLUE	BARBECUE
FIRE	DOUBLE	FREE SPACE	SPY	BOOK
FUN	FIGHT	CHURCH	SODAPOP	GOOD
HAIRCUT	THEME	JOHNNY	CHERRY	PRIDE

The Outsiders

HAIRCUT	JOHNNY	JUDGE	SMOKE	CHURCH
CHERRY	GREASERS	SPY	TWO	FOUNTAIN
CIGARETTES	BLUE	FREE SPACE	FIRE	BOOK
RUMBLE	HOSPITAL	DOUBLE	BARBECUE	GOLDEN
PONYBOY	GALLANT	DARRY	GOOD	TRAIN

The Outsiders

BROTHERS	COKE	JACKET	PAUL	TIM
PRIDE	OUTSIDERS	HINTON	RINGS	LOT
SOCS	BOB	FREE SPACE	NEWSPAPER	DALLAS
FUN	SODAPOP	FROST	MUSTANG	GUN
ARM	THEME	MARCIA	BLOOD	MOTHER

The Outsiders

BLOOD	COKE	RUMBLE	SOCS	DALLAS
SPY	THEME	JACKET	TIM	FIRE
RINGS	CIGARETTES	FREE SPACE	TURF	CHURCH
HAIRCUT	FOUNTAIN	CHERRY	SMOKE	GOLDEN
BLADE	RANDY	OUTSIDERS	HINTON	FUN

The Outsiders

GALLANT	MOTHER	DARRY	KNIFE	GREASERS
PAUL	BROTHERS	SODAPOP	BOTTLE	BLUE
TRAIN	LATE	FREE SPACE	TWO	BOB
DEAD	LOT	PRIDE	MUSTANG	ARM
PONYBOY	HOSPITAL	DOUBLE	FROST	NEWSPAPER

The Outsiders

KNIFE	GOLDEN	PAUL	SOCS	BLADE
BOTTLE	DOUBLE	TURF	PRIDE	JACKET
FIGHT	DARRY	FREE SPACE	THEME	SPY
PONYBOY	OUTSIDERS	TIM	FIRE	WINSTON
CHURCH	HINTON	RANDY	FROST	TRAIN

The Outsiders

MARCIA	FUN	MOTHER	HAIRCUT	CIGARETTES
HOSPITAL	FOUNTAIN	DEAD	BLOOD	BOB
LATE	JOHNNY	FREE SPACE	GREASERS	BARBECUE
GOOD	RUMBLE	DALLAS	SMOKE	BLUE
LOT	MOUNTAIN	NEWSPAPER	GUN	TWO

The Outsiders

NEWSPAPER	HAIRCUT	TIM	BLADE	BOOK
TURF	DARRY	BARBECUE	COKE	PAUL
GREASERS	CHERRY	FREE SPACE	GALLANT	MOTHER
JACKET	FIRE	HOSPITAL	HINTON	KNIFE
JUDGE	BOTTLE	SODAPOP	CIGARETTES	TWO

The Outsiders

SPY	MUSTANG	OUTSIDERS	TRAIN	DOUBLE
GUN	DEAD	MOUNTAIN	FUN	FROST
FIGHT	RUMBLE	FREE SPACE	JOHNNY	PRIDE
ARM	RINGS	FOUNTAIN	GOLDEN	BLOOD
THEME	BROTHERS	LATE	LOT	MARCIA

The Outsiders

WINSTON	OUTSIDERS	THEME	GALLANT	FROST
SPY	RINGS	SOCS	BOB	FOUNTAIN
PRIDE	CIGARETTES	FREE SPACE	BLADE	FUN
FIRE	HINTON	DARRY	GOOD	PONYBOY
BOTTLE	MARCIA	KNIFE	CHURCH	JUDGE

The Outsiders

SODAPOP	GREASERS	BROTHERS	DALLAS	RUMBLE
CHERRY	COKE	LATE	BLUE	MUSTANG
NEWSPAPER	TIM	FREE SPACE	TURF	BOOK
JACKET	JOHNNY	LOT	MOUNTAIN	GUN
DEAD	GOLDEN	TRAIN	DOUBLE	TWO

The Outsiders

DALLAS	BLADE	JUDGE	OUTSIDERS	BOTTLE
WINSTON	DOUBLE	MUSTANG	MARCIA	BARBECUE
TURF	RUMBLE	FREE SPACE	FROST	CHURCH
GALLANT	RINGS	BOB	PAUL	LATE
LOT	DARRY	GOOD	PRIDE	MOTHER

The Outsiders

NEWSPAPER	SPY	KNIFE	GREASERS	SODAPOP
HOSPITAL	ARM	TRAIN	PONYBOY	BOOK
BLUE	TIM	FREE SPACE	CHERRY	SOCS
COKE	FOUNTAIN	FIRE	BLOOD	RANDY
MOUNTAIN	FIGHT	TWO	DEAD	HAIRCUT

The Outsiders Vocabulary Word List

No.	Word	Clue/Definition
1.	ABRUPTLY	suddenly
2.	ACQUITTED	discharged completely, set free from a legal charge
3.	AGHAST	amazed, stupefied
4.	AIMLESSLY	without direction, without purpose
5.	APPREHENSIVE	afraid, suspicious
6.	ASSET	worth
7.	BEWILDERDLY	confusedly
8.	BEWILDERING	confused, perplexed
9.	BOOTLEGGING	selling alcohol where not legally available
10.	COMPLICATED	involved, complex
11.	CONTEMPTUOUSLY	scornful, insolent
12.	CONTENT	satisfied, pleased
13.	CONVICTION	strong belief
14.	COWLICK	tuft of hair growing in a different direction
15.	DEBATING	deciding
16.	DELIRIOUS	confusion, disordered speech, hallucinations
17.	DESPERATE	driven to take any risk
18.	ELITE	a select body, the best
19.	ELUDED	escaped, avoided
20.	EXPLOITS	heroic acts, adventures
21.	FLINCHING	betraying fear, pain or surprise with an involuntary gesture
22.	GORGED	swallow with greediness
23.	GRASPED	understood
24.	GROGGY	not fully awake
25.	IMPLORINGLY	beesechingly
26.	INCREDULOUS	unbelieving
27.	INDIGNANT	disgusted, anger with contempt
28.	INHALATION	to breathe into the lungs
29.	LEERY	wary, suspicious
30.	LONED	by oneself
31.	MADRAS	cotton fabric shirt usually brightly colored
32.	MIMICKING	imitating, ridiculing
33.	NONCHALANTLY	indifferently
34.	PITY	compassion for suffering
35.	PREMONITION	previous warning, information, feeling
36.	QUIVERING	trembling, shaking
37.	RARELY	uncommon, infrequent
38.	RECURRING	returning, repeatedly
39.	RELUCTANTLY	unwillingly, struggling
40.	RESIGNEDLY	giving up, accepting the future
41.	RESEMBLANCE	likeness, similarity
42.	RUEFULLY	regretfully, sorrowfully
43.	SARCASM	bitter cutting jest
44.	SLOUCHED	an ungainly gait
45.	SOPHISTICATED	cultured, worldly
46.	STUPOR	senses are deadened
47.	SULLENLY	gloomily, somber
48.	VEERED	swerved, turned aside from a course or direction
49.	VITAL	essential, necessary to life
50.	WINCED	to shrink back as if from pain

The Outsiders Vocabulary Fill In The Blank 1

_____ 1. worth

_____ 2. swerved, turned aside from a course or direction

_____ 3. senses are deadened

_____ 4. beesechingly

_____ 5. compassion for suffering

_____ 6. uncommon, infrequent

_____ 7. indifferently

_____ 8. by oneself

_____ 9. giving up, accepting the future

_____ 10. discharged completely, set free from a legal charge

_____ 11. to shrink back as if from pain

_____ 12. driven to take any risk

_____ 13. regretfully, sorrowfully

_____ 14. to breathe into the lungs

_____ 15. confused, perplexed

_____ 16. confusedly

_____ 17. an ungainly gait

_____ 18. disgusted, anger with contempt

_____ 19. a select body, the best

_____ 20. deciding

The Outsiders Vocabulary Fill In The Blank 1 Answer Key

ASSET	1. worth
VEERED	2. swerved, turned aside from a course or direction
STUPOR	3. senses are deadened
IMPLORINGLY	4. beesechingly
PITY	5. compassion for suffering
RARELY	6. uncommon, infrequent
NONCHALANTLY	7. indifferently
LONED	8. by oneself
RESIGNEDLY	9. giving up, accepting the future
ACQUITTED	10. discharged completely, set free from a legal charge
WINCED	11. to shrink back as if from pain
DESPERATE	12. driven to take any risk
RUEFULLY	13. regretfully, sorrowfully
INHALATION	14. to breathe into the lungs
BEWILDERING	15. confused, perplexed
BEWILDERDLY	16. confusedly
SLOUCHED	17. an ungainly gait
INDIGNANT	18. disgusted, anger with contempt
ELITE	19. a select body, the best
DEBATING	20. deciding

The Outsiders Vocabulary Fill In The Blank 2

_____ 1. an ungainly gait
_____ 2. senses are deadened
_____ 3. deciding
_____ 4. to breathe into the lungs
_____ 5. swallow with greediness
_____ 6. disgusted, anger with contempt
_____ 7. satisfied, pleased
_____ 8. returning, repeatedly
_____ 9. by oneself
_____ 10. unbelieving
_____ 11. gloomily, somber
_____ 12. a select body, the best
_____ 13. afraid, suspicious
_____ 14. driven to take any risk
_____ 15. indifferently
_____ 16. swerved, turned aside from a course or direction
_____ 17. suddenly
_____ 18. previous warning, information, feeling
_____ 19. uncommon, infrequent
_____ 20. heroic acts, adventures

The Outsiders Vocabulary Fill In The Blank 2 Answer Key

SLOUCHED	1. an ungainly gait
STUPOR	2. senses are deadened
DEBATING	3. deciding
INHALATION	4. to breathe into the lungs
GORGED	5. swallow with greediness
INDIGNANT	6. disgusted, anger with contempt
CONTENT	7. satisfied, pleased
RECURRING	8. returning, repeatedly
LONED	9. by oneself
INCREDULOUS	10. unbelieving
SULLENLY	11. gloomily, somber
ELITE	12. a select body, the best
APPREHENSIVE	13. afraid, suspicious
DESPERATE	14. driven to take any risk
NONCHALANTLY	15. indifferently
VEERED	16. swerved, turned aside from a course or direction
ABRUPTLY	17. suddenly
PREMONITION	18. previous warning, information, feeling
RARELY	19. uncommon, infrequent
EXPLOITS	20. heroic acts, adventures

The Outsiders Vocabulary Fill In The Blank 3

_____ 1. previous warning, information, feeling

_____ 2. deciding

_____ 3. a select body, the best

_____ 4. involved, complex

_____ 5. strong belief

_____ 6. senses are deadened

_____ 7. scornful, insolent

_____ 8. indifferently

_____ 9. wary, suspicious

_____ 10. not fully awake

_____ 11. selling alcohol where not legally available

_____ 12. discharged completely, set free from a legal charge

_____ 13. likeness, similarity

_____ 14. confusion, disordered speech, hallucinations

_____ 15. giving up, accepting the future

_____ 16. gloomily, somber

_____ 17. understood

_____ 18. swallow with greediness

_____ 19. trembling, shaking

_____ 20. to shrink back as if from pain

The Outsiders Vocabulary Fill In The Blank 3 Answer Key

PREMONITION	1. previous warning, information, feeling
DEBATING	2. deciding
ELITE	3. a select body, the best
COMPLICATED	4. involved, complex
CONVICTION	5. strong belief
STUPOR	6. senses are deadened
CONTEMPTUOUSLY	7. scornful, insolent
NONCHALANTLY	8. indifferently
LEERY	9. wary, suspicious
GROGGY	10. not fully awake
BOOTLEGGING	11. selling alcohol where not legally available
ACQUITTED	12. discharged completely, set free from a legal charge
RESEMBLANCE	13. likeness, similarity
DELIRIOUS	14. confusion, disordered speech, hallucinations
RESIGNEDLY	15. giving up, accepting the future
SULLENLY	16. gloomily, somber
GRASPED	17. understood
GORGED	18. swallow with greediness
QUIVERING	19. trembling, shaking
WINCED	20. to shrink back as if from pain

The Outsiders Vocabulary Fill In The Blank 4

1. compassion for suffering
2. involved, complex
3. disgusted, anger with contempt
4. amazed, stupefied
5. to breathe into the lungs
6. strong belief
7. senses are deadened
8. essential, necessary to life
9. previous warning, information, feeling
10. returning, repeatedly
11. deciding
12. scornful, insolent
13. cultured, worldly
14. without direction, without purpose
15. indifferently
16. gloomily, somber
17. discharged completely, set free from a legal charge
18. not fully awake
19. bitter cutting jest
20. worth

The Outsiders Vocabulary Fill In The Blank 4 Answer Key

PITY	1.	compassion for suffering
COMPLICATED	2.	involved, complex
INDIGNANT	3.	disgusted, anger with contempt
AGHAST	4.	amazed, stupefied
INHALATION	5.	to breathe into the lungs
CONVICTION	6.	strong belief
STUPOR	7.	senses are deadened
VITAL	8.	essential, necessary to life
PREMONITION	9.	previous warning, information, feeling
RECURRING	10.	returning, repeatedly
DEBATING	11.	deciding
CONTEMPTUOUSLY	12.	scornful, insolent
SOPHISTICATED	13.	cultured, worldly
AIMLESSLY	14.	without direction, without purpose
NONCHALANTLY	15.	indifferently
SULLENLY	16.	gloomily, somber
ACQUITTED	17.	discharged completely, set free from a legal charge
GROGGY	18.	not fully awake
SARCASM	19.	bitter cutting jest
ASSET	20.	worth

The Outsiders Vocabulary Matching 1

___ 1. RECURRING   A. an ungainly gait
___ 2. INCREDULOUS   B. worth
___ 3. ELUDED   C. cultured, worldly
___ 4. LEERY   D. swallow with greediness
___ 5. DESPERATE   E. escaped, avoided
___ 6. CONVICTION   F. indifferently
___ 7. SLOUCHED   G. imitating, ridiculing
___ 8. SOPHISTICATED   H. returning, repeatedly
___ 9. PITY   I. unbelieving
___10. INDIGNANT   J. wary, suspicious
___11. AIMLESSLY   K. giving up, accepting the future
___12. ASSET   L. without direction, without purpose
___13. ABRUPTLY   M. unwillingly, struggling
___14. GORGED   N. bitter cutting jest
___15. MIMICKING   O. disgusted, anger with contempt
___16. MADRAS   P. suddenly
___17. RELUCTANTLY   Q. regretfully, sorrowfully
___18. NONCHALANTLY   R. beesechingly
___19. IMPLORINGLY   S. likeness, similarity
___20. BEWILDERING   T. compassion for suffering
___21. RUEFULLY   U. confused, perplexed
___22. RESIGNEDLY   V. strong belief
___23. RESEMBLANCE   W. cotton fabric shirt usually brightly colored
___24. CONTEMPTUOUSLY   X. scornful, insolent
___25. SARCASM   Y. driven to take any risk

The Outsiders Vocabulary Matching 1 Answer Key

H - 1. RECURRING	A.	an ungainly gait
I - 2. INCREDULOUS	B.	worth
E - 3. ELUDED	C.	cultured, worldly
J - 4. LEERY	D.	swallow with greediness
Y - 5. DESPERATE	E.	escaped, avoided
V - 6. CONVICTION	F.	indifferently
A - 7. SLOUCHED	G.	imitating, ridiculing
C - 8. SOPHISTICATED	H.	returning, repeatedly
T - 9. PITY	I.	unbelieving
O -10. INDIGNANT	J.	wary, suspicious
L -11. AIMLESSLY	K.	giving up, accepting the future
B -12. ASSET	L.	without direction, without purpose
P -13. ABRUPTLY	M.	unwillingly, struggling
D -14. GORGED	N.	bitter cutting jest
G -15. MIMICKING	O.	disgusted, anger with contempt
W -16. MADRAS	P.	suddenly
M -17. RELUCTANTLY	Q.	regretfully, sorrowfully
F -18. NONCHALANTLY	R.	beesechingly
R -19. IMPLORINGLY	S.	likeness, similarity
U -20. BEWILDERING	T.	compassion for suffering
Q -21. RUEFULLY	U.	confused, perplexed
K -22. RESIGNEDLY	V.	strong belief
S -23. RESEMBLANCE	W.	cotton fabric shirt usually brightly colored
X -24. CONTEMPTUOUSLY	X.	scornful, insolent
N -25. SARCASM	Y.	driven to take any risk

The Outsiders Vocabulary Matching 2

___ 1. COWLICK   A. confusedly
___ 2. STUPOR   B. bitter cutting jest
___ 3. INDIGNANT   C. senses are deadened
___ 4. ELUDED   D. cultured, worldly
___ 5. MADRAS   E. satisfied, pleased
___ 6. RUEFULLY   F. driven to take any risk
___ 7. BEWILDERDLY   G. gloomily, somber
___ 8. RECURRING   H. tuft of hair growing in a different direction
___ 9. SULLENLY   I. swallow with greediness
___10. DESPERATE   J. unbelieving
___11. VITAL   K. escaped, avoided
___12. CONTENT   L. strong belief
___13. RELUCTANTLY   M. unwillingly, struggling
___14. ACQUITTED   N. understood
___15. CONVICTION   O. regretfully, sorrowfully
___16. QUIVERING   P. returning, repeatedly
___17. INHALATION   Q. essential, necessary to life
___18. SARCASM   R. disgusted, anger with contempt
___19. GRASPED   S. discharged completely, set free from a legal charge
___20. INCREDULOUS   T. suddenly
___21. SLOUCHED   U. cotton fabric shirt usually brightly colored
___22. ABRUPTLY   V. an ungainly gait
___23. IMPLORINGLY   W. to breathe into the lungs
___24. GORGED   X. trembling, shaking
___25. SOPHISTICATED   Y. beesechingly

The Outsiders Vocabulary Matching 2 Answer Key

H - 1. COWLICK		A. confusedly
C - 2. STUPOR		B. bitter cutting jest
R - 3. INDIGNANT		C. senses are deadened
K - 4. ELUDED		D. cultured, worldly
U - 5. MADRAS		E. satisfied, pleased
O - 6. RUEFULLY		F. driven to take any risk
A - 7. BEWILDERDLY		G. gloomily, somber
P - 8. RECURRING		H. tuft of hair growing in a different direction
G - 9. SULLENLY		I. swallow with greediness
F - 10. DESPERATE		J. unbelieving
Q - 11. VITAL		K. escaped, avoided
E - 12. CONTENT		L. strong belief
M - 13. RELUCTANTLY		M. unwillingly, struggling
S - 14. ACQUITTED		N. understood
L - 15. CONVICTION		O. regretfully, sorrowfully
X - 16. QUIVERING		P. returning, repeatedly
W - 17. INHALATION		Q. essential, necessary to life
B - 18. SARCASM		R. disgusted, anger with contempt
N - 19. GRASPED		S. discharged completely, set free from a legal charge
J - 20. INCREDULOUS		T. suddenly
V - 21. SLOUCHED		U. cotton fabric shirt usually brightly colored
T - 22. ABRUPTLY		V. an ungainly gait
Y - 23. IMPLORINGLY		W. to breathe into the lungs
I - 24. GORGED		X. trembling, shaking
D - 25. SOPHISTICATED		Y. beesechingly

The Outsiders Vocabulary Matching 3

___ 1. INCREDULOUS   A. unbelieving
___ 2. MADRAS   B. worth
___ 3. NONCHALANTLY   C. selling alcohol where not legally available
___ 4. EXPLOITS   D. trembling, shaking
___ 5. QUIVERING   E. escaped, avoided
___ 6. CONTEMPTUOUSLY   F. cotton fabric shirt usually brightly colored
___ 7. BOOTLEGGING   G. by oneself
___ 8. INHALATION   H. uncommon, infrequent
___ 9. CONTENT   I. swallow with greediness
___10. SOPHISTICATED   J. heroic acts, adventures
___11. BEWILDERDLY   K. scornful, insolent
___12. FLINCHING   L. to breathe into the lungs
___13. ASSET   M. likeness, similarity
___14. RARELY   N. cultured, worldly
___15. AGHAST   O. senses are deadened
___16. LEERY   P. confusedly
___17. ELITE   Q. unwillingly, struggling
___18. RELUCTANTLY   R. betraying fear, pain or surprise with an involuntary gesture
___19. INDIGNANT   S. disgusted, anger with contempt
___20. LONED   T. satisfied, pleased
___21. RESEMBLANCE   U. indifferently
___22. ELUDED   V. amazed, stupefied
___23. COMPLICATED   W. involved, complex
___24. GORGED   X. wary, suspicious
___25. STUPOR   Y. a select body, the best

The Outsiders Vocabulary Matching 3 Answer Key

A - 1. INCREDULOUS	A.	unbelieving
F - 2. MADRAS	B.	worth
U - 3. NONCHALANTLY	C.	selling alcohol where not legally available
J - 4. EXPLOITS	D.	trembling, shaking
D - 5. QUIVERING	E.	escaped, avoided
K - 6. CONTEMPTUOUSLY	F.	cotton fabric shirt usually brightly colored
C - 7. BOOTLEGGING	G.	by oneself
L - 8. INHALATION	H.	uncommon, infrequent
T - 9. CONTENT	I.	swallow with greediness
N -10. SOPHISTICATED	J.	heroic acts, adventures
P -11. BEWILDERDLY	K.	scornful, insolent
R -12. FLINCHING	L.	to breathe into the lungs
B -13. ASSET	M.	likeness, similarity
H -14. RARELY	N.	cultured, worldly
V -15. AGHAST	O.	senses are deadened
X -16. LEERY	P.	confusedly
Y -17. ELITE	Q.	unwillingly, struggling
Q -18. RELUCTANTLY	R.	betraying fear, pain or surprise with an involuntary gesture
S -19. INDIGNANT	S.	disgusted, anger with contempt
G -20. LONED	T.	satisfied, pleased
M -21. RESEMBLANCE	U.	indifferently
E -22. ELUDED	V.	amazed, stupefied
W -23. COMPLICATED	W.	involved, complex
I -24. GORGED	X.	wary, suspicious
O -25. STUPOR	Y.	a select body, the best

The Outsiders Vocabulary Matching 4

___ 1. BEWILDERING   A. cotton fabric shirt usually brightly colored
___ 2. SOPHISTICATED   B. worth
___ 3. GROGGY   C. wary, suspicious
___ 4. SULLENLY   D. essential, necessary to life
___ 5. DESPERATE   E. confusion, disordered speech, hallucinations
___ 6. ASSET   F. understood
___ 7. COWLICK   G. senses are deadened
___ 8. CONTEMPTUOUSLY   H. deciding
___ 9. MADRAS   I. a select body, the best
___ 10. BOOTLEGGING   J. not fully awake
___ 11. EXPLOITS   K. gloomily, somber
___ 12. MIMICKING   L. indifferently
___ 13. INCREDULOUS   M. scornful, insolent
___ 14. RESIGNEDLY   N. tuft of hair growing in a different direction
___ 15. DELIRIOUS   O. heroic acts, adventures
___ 16. VITAL   P. selling alcohol where not legally available
___ 17. CONTENT   Q. swerved, turned aside from a course or direction
___ 18. NONCHALANTLY   R. without direction, without purpose
___ 19. VEERED   S. cultured, worldly
___ 20. GRASPED   T. imitating, ridiculing
___ 21. DEBATING   U. satisfied, pleased
___ 22. AIMLESSLY   V. unbelieving
___ 23. STUPOR   W. driven to take any risk
___ 24. ELITE   X. giving up, accepting the future
___ 25. LEERY   Y. confused, perplexed

The Outsiders Vocabulary Matching 4 Answer Key

Y - 1.	BEWILDERING	A. cotton fabric shirt usually brightly colored
S - 2.	SOPHISTICATED	B. worth
J - 3.	GROGGY	C. wary, suspicious
K - 4.	SULLENLY	D. essential, necessary to life
W - 5.	DESPERATE	E. confusion, disordered speech, hallucinations
B - 6.	ASSET	F. understood
N - 7.	COWLICK	G. senses are deadened
M - 8.	CONTEMPTUOUSLY	H. deciding
A - 9.	MADRAS	I. a select body, the best
P - 10.	BOOTLEGGING	J. not fully awake
O - 11.	EXPLOITS	K. gloomily, somber
T - 12.	MIMICKING	L. indifferently
V - 13.	INCREDULOUS	M. scornful, insolent
X - 14.	RESIGNEDLY	N. tuft of hair growing in a different direction
E - 15.	DELIRIOUS	O. heroic acts, adventures
D - 16.	VITAL	P. selling alcohol where not legally available
U - 17.	CONTENT	Q. swerved, turned aside from a course or direction
L - 18.	NONCHALANTLY	R. without direction, without purpose
Q - 19.	VEERED	S. cultured, worldly
F - 20.	GRASPED	T. imitating, ridiculing
H - 21.	DEBATING	U. satisfied, pleased
R - 22.	AIMLESSLY	V. unbelieving
G - 23.	STUPOR	W. driven to take any risk
I - 24.	ELITE	X. giving up, accepting the future
C - 25.	LEERY	Y. confused, perplexed

The Outsiders Vocabulary Magic Squares 1

Match the definition with the vocabulary word. Put your answers in the magic squares below. When your answers are correct, all columns and rows will add to the same number.

A. LONED
B. ELUDED
C. SOPHISTICATED
D. ELITE
E. SULLENLY
F. DESPERATE
G. PREMONITION
H. CONTEMPTUOUSLY
I. RELUCTANTLY
J. AGHAST
K. MIMICKING
L. PITY
M. GORGED
N. GROGGY
O. AIMLESSLY
P. CONVICTION

1. cultured, worldly
2. amazed, stupefied
3. driven to take any risk
4. without direction, without purpose
5. strong belief
6. gloomily, somber
7. unwillingly, struggling
8. a select body, the best
9. swallow with greediness
10. scornful, insolent
11. compassion for suffering
12. by oneself
13. escaped, avoided
14. imitating, ridiculing
15. previous warning, information, feeling
16. not fully awake

A=	B=	C=	D=
E=	F=	G=	H=
I=	J=	K=	L=
M=	N=	O=	P=

The Outsiders Vocabulary Magic Squares 1 Answer Key

Match the definition with the vocabulary word. Put your answers in the magic squares below. When your answers are correct, all columns and rows will add to the same number.

A. LONED
B. ELUDED
C. SOPHISTICATED
D. ELITE
E. SULLENLY
F. DESPERATE
G. PREMONITION
H. CONTEMPTUOUSLY
I. RELUCTANTLY
J. AGHAST
K. MIMICKING
L. PITY
M. GORGED
N. GROGGY
O. AIMLESSLY
P. CONVICTION

1. cultured, worldly
2. amazed, stupefied
3. driven to take any risk
4. without direction, without purpose
5. strong belief
6. gloomily, somber
7. unwillingly, struggling
8. a select body, the best
9. swallow with greediness
10. scornful, insolent
11. compassion for suffering
12. by oneself
13. escaped, avoided
14. imitating, ridiculing
15. previous warning, information, feeling
16. not fully awake

A=12	B=13	C=1	D=8
E=6	F=3	G=15	H=10
I=7	J=2	K=14	L=11
M=9	N=16	O=4	P=5

The Outsiders Vocabulary Magic Squares 2

Match the definition with the vocabulary word. Put your answers in the magic squares below. When your answers are correct, all columns and rows will add to the same number.

A. PREMONITION
B. GROGGY
C. RESEMBLANCE
D. COMPLICATED
E. SARCASM
F. SULLENLY
G. GORGED
H. AGHAST
I. MADRAS
J. LONED
K. ASSET
L. MIMICKING
M. SLOUCHED
N. VITAL
O. BEWILDERDLY
P. ACQUITTED

1. gloomily, somber
2. cotton fabric shirt usually brightly colored
3. confusedly
4. involved, complex
5. an ungainly gait
6. not fully awake
7. amazed, stupefied
8. worth
9. likeness, similarity
10. discharged completely, set free from a legal charge
11. by oneself
12. bitter cutting jest
13. imitating, ridiculing
14. swallow with greediness
15. previous warning, information, feeling
16. essential, necessary to life

A=	B=	C=	D=
E=	F=	G=	H=
I=	J=	K=	L=
M=	N=	O=	P=

The Outsiders Vocabulary Magic Squares 2 Answer Key

Match the definition with the vocabulary word. Put your answers in the magic squares below. When your answers are correct, all columns and rows will add to the same number.

A. PREMONITION
B. GROGGY
C. RESEMBLANCE
D. COMPLICATED
E. SARCASM
F. SULLENLY
G. GORGED
H. AGHAST
I. MADRAS
J. LONED
K. ASSET
L. MIMICKING
M. SLOUCHED
N. VITAL
O. BEWILDERDLY
P. ACQUITTED

1. gloomily, somber
2. cotton fabric shirt usually brightly colored
3. confusedly
4. involved, complex
5. an ungainly gait
6. not fully awake
7. amazed, stupefied
8. worth
9. likeness, similarity
10. discharged completely, set free from a legal charge
11. by oneself
12. bitter cutting jest
13. imitating, ridiculing
14. swallow with greediness
15. previous warning, information, feeling
16. essential, necessary to life

A=15	B=6	C=9	D=4
E=12	F=1	G=14	H=7
I=2	J=11	K=8	L=13
M=5	N=16	O=3	P=10

The Outsiders Vocabulary Magic Squares 3

Match the definition with the vocabulary word. Put your answers in the magic squares below. When your answers are correct, all columns and rows will add to the same number.

A. VEERED
B. GROGGY
C. DESPERATE
D. AIMLESSLY
E. RECURRING
F. GRASPED
G. SOPHISTICATED
H. COMPLICATED
I. FLINCHING
J. AGHAST
K. MADRAS
L. APPREHENSIVE
M. ELITE
N. SULLENLY
O. RARELY
P. BEWILDERDLY

1. not fully awake
2. cultured, worldly
3. cotton fabric shirt usually brightly colored
4. gloomily, somber
5. a select body, the best
6. afraid, suspicious
7. involved, complex
8. swerved, turned aside from a course or direction
9. confusedly
10. betraying fear, pain or surprise with an involuntary gesture
11. returning, repeatedly
12. without direction, without purpose
13. driven to take any risk
14. understood
15. amazed, stupefied
16. uncommon, infrequent

A=	B=	C=	D=
E=	F=	G=	H=
I=	J=	K=	L=
M=	N=	O=	P=

The Outsiders Vocabulary Magic Squares 3 Answer Key

Match the definition with the vocabulary word. Put your answers in the magic squares below. When your answers are correct, all columns and rows will add to the same number.

A. VEERED
B. GROGGY
C. DESPERATE
D. AIMLESSLY
E. RECURRING
F. GRASPED
G. SOPHISTICATED
H. COMPLICATED
I. FLINCHING
J. AGHAST
K. MADRAS
L. APPREHENSIVE
M. ELITE
N. SULLENLY
O. RARELY
P. BEWILDERDLY

1. not fully awake
2. cultured, worldly
3. cotton fabric shirt usually brightly colored
4. gloomily, somber
5. a select body, the best
6. afraid, suspicious
7. involved, complex
8. swerved, turned aside from a course or direction
9. confusedly
10. betraying fear, pain or surprise with an involuntary gesture
11. returning, repeatedly
12. without direction, without purpose
13. driven to take any risk
14. understood
15. amazed, stupefied
16. uncommon, infrequent

A=8	B=1	C=13	D=12
E=11	F=14	G=2	H=7
I=10	J=15	K=3	L=6
M=5	N=4	O=16	P=9

The Outsiders Vocabulary Magic Squares 4

Match the definition with the vocabulary word. Put your answers in the magic squares below. When your answers are correct, all columns and rows will add to the same number.

A. COMPLICATED
B. VEERED
C. FLINCHING
D. BEWILDERDLY
E. DELIRIOUS
F. CONVICTION
G. GORGED
H. SLOUCHED
I. ELITE
J. VITAL
K. ACQUITTED
L. PREMONITION
M. NONCHALANTLY
N. DEBATING
O. PITY
P. RELUCTANTLY

1. involved, complex
2. deciding
3. essential, necessary to life
4. confusion, disordered speech, hallucinations
5. swallow with greediness
6. previous warning, information, feeling
7. unwillingly, struggling
8. betraying fear, pain or surprise with an involuntary gesture
9. compassion for suffering
10. confusedly
11. an ungainly gait
12. discharged completely, set free from a legal charge
13. a select body, the best
14. strong belief
15. swerved, turned aside from a course or direction
16. indifferently

A=	B=	C=	D=
E=	F=	G=	H=
I=	J=	K=	L=
M=	N=	O=	P=

The Outsiders Vocabulary Magic Squares 4 Answer Key

Match the definition with the vocabulary word. Put your answers in the magic squares below. When your answers are correct, all columns and rows will add to the same number.

A. COMPLICATED
B. VEERED
C. FLINCHING
D. BEWILDERDLY
E. DELIRIOUS
F. CONVICTION
G. GORGED
H. SLOUCHED
I. ELITE
J. VITAL
K. ACQUITTED
L. PREMONITION
M. NONCHALANTLY
N. DEBATING
O. PITY
P. RELUCTANTLY

1. involved, complex
2. deciding
3. essential, necessary to life
4. confusion, disordered speech, hallucinations
5. swallow with greediness
6. previous warning, information, feeling
7. unwillingly, struggling
8. betraying fear, pain or surprise with an involuntary gesture
9. compassion for suffering
10. confusedly
11. an ungainly gait
12. discharged completely, set free from a legal charge
13. a select body, the best
14. strong belief
15. swerved, turned aside from a course or direction
16. indifferently

A=1	B=15	C=8	D=10
E=4	F=14	G=5	H=11
I=13	J=3	K=12	L=6
M=16	N=2	O=9	P=7

The Outsiders Vocabulary Word Search 1

```
G O R G E D F V R F L I N C H I N G P D
N O I T I N O M E R P G D L G Q M R D P
A S B N C M G J C T S C E X B X Y A A N
F I J Z J O M D U M M D S D X G L S S V
S R M N M S N Z R V A N P U G Y V P S G
M A R L D D C V R D T D E O L L S E E E
T I R D E L I R I O U S R S R L K D T D
F N Q C T S V A N C X G A A E U E I S B
P D N R A S S I G L T Z T W S F L N S D
P I R Y C S O L T H O I E G E E Q R L M
W G T E I B M P Y A A N O W M U U A O Y
R N C Y L Y I C H L L S E N B R I R U T
E A O D P U N S O I N F T D L W V E C K
S N W E M X C H T N S Z S Y A A E L H G
I T L B O V R T Y U T T R C N B R Y E N
G W I A C E E F A S P E I Z C R I D D F
N L C T N E D B M N E O N C E U N L Z G
E V K I V R U C Y L T F R T A P G P N R
D H M N Z E L S T I O L P X E T Y X P K
L P K G G D O C F C G S Y L C L E D P L
Y Y L S U O T P M E T N O C Y L D P P F
E L U D E D S M I M I C K I N G V V Z J
```

a select body, the best (5)
amazed, stupefied (6)
an ungainly gait (8)
betraying fear, pain or surprise with an involuntary gesture (9)
bitter cutting jest (7)
by oneself (5)
compassion for suffering (4)
confusion, disordered speech, hallucinations (9)
cotton fabric shirt usually brightly colored (6)
cultured, worldly (13)
deciding (8)
disgusted, anger with contempt (9)
driven to take any risk (9)
escaped, avoided (6)
essential, necessary to life (5)
giving up, accepting the future (10)
gloomily, somber (8)
heroic acts, adventures (8)
imitating, ridiculing (9)
involved, complex (11)
likeness, similarity (11)
not fully awake (6)

previous warning, information, feeling (11)
regretfully, sorrowfully (8)
returning, repeatedly (9)
satisfied, pleased (7)
scornful, insolent (14)
senses are deadened (6)
strong belief (10)
suddenly (8)
swallow with greediness (6)
swerved, turned aside from a course or direction (6)
to shrink back as if from pain (6)
trembling, shaking (9)
tuft of hair growing in a different direction (7)
unbelieving (11)
uncommon, infrequent (6)
understood (7)
unwillingly, struggling (11)
wary, suspicious (5)
without direction, without purpose (9)
worth (5)

The Outsiders Vocabulary Word Search 1 Answer Key

```
G   O   R   G   E   D           R   F   L   I   N   C   H   I   N   G
N   O   I   T   I   N   O   M   E   R   P           D                   R
A                   C                   C                   E               Y   A   A
        I                   O                   U   M           S               G       S   S
S       M                       N           R           A       P   U   G   Y       P   S
        A       L   D   D           V   R               D   E   O   L   L       E   E   E
        I   R   D   E   L   I   R   I   O   U   S   R       R   L           D   T
        N           C   T   S   V   A   N   C       G   A   A   E   U   E   I
P   D   N           A   S   S   I   G   L   T           T       S   F   L   N   S
    I   R           C   S   O   L   T   H   O   I   E       E   E   Q   R   L
W   G   T   E   I       M   P   Y   A   A   N   O           M   U   U   A   O   Y
R   N   C   Y   L       I       C   H           L   S   E   N   B   R   I   R   U
E   A   O   D   P   U   N   S   O   I                   T   D   L       V   E   C
S   N   W   E   M           C           T   N   S               Y   A   A   E   L   H
I   T   L   B   O   V   R   T               U   T   T   R           N   B   R   Y   E
G       I   A   C   E   E           A           P   E   I           C   R   I       D
N       C   T       E   D               N   E   O   N   C   E   U   N
E       K   I       R   U                   L   T       R   T   A   P   G
D           N       E   L   S   T   I   O   L   P   X   E   T
L           G       D   O                       Y               L   E
Y   Y   L   S   U   O   U   T   P   M   E   T   N   O   C   Y       D
E   L   U   D   E   D   S   M   I   M   I   C   K   I   N   G
```

a select body, the best (5)
amazed, stupefied (6)
an ungainly gait (8)
betraying fear, pain or surprise with an involuntary gesture (9)
bitter cutting jest (7)
by oneself (5)
compassion for suffering (4)
confusion, disordered speech, hallucinations (9)
cotton fabric shirt usually brightly colored (6)
cultured, worldly (13)
deciding (8)
disgusted, anger with contempt (9)
driven to take any risk (9)
escaped, avoided (6)
essential, necessary to life (5)
giving up, accepting the future (10)
gloomily, somber (8)
heroic acts, adventures (8)
imitating, ridiculing (9)
involved, complex (11)
likeness, similarity (11)
not fully awake (6)

previous warning, information, feeling (11)
regretfully, sorrowfully (8)
returning, repeatedly (9)
satisfied, pleased (7)
scornful, insolent (14)
senses are deadened (6)
strong belief (10)
suddenly (8)
swallow with greediness (6)
swerved, turned aside from a course or direction (6)
to shrink back as if from pain (6)
trembling, shaking (9)
tuft of hair growing in a different direction (7)
unbelieving (11)
uncommon, infrequent (6)
understood (7)
unwillingly, struggling (11)
wary, suspicious (5)
without direction, without purpose (9)
worth (5)

The Outsiders Vocabulary Word Search 2

```
R E S E M B L A N C E D E B A T I N G R
E W S U L L E N L Y E X W C B G M B N C
L A I V Z U F N L S W R Q M R R P W I K
U P Z N D J D D P Y Y U G T U O L C G S
C P P S C X V E M R I E D P P G O R G N
T R T F Y E R A D T X E E Q T G R K E N
A E R T X A D Z T P R D T B L Y I Z L X
N H B Z T R C E L E W B A E Y K N R T D
T E E E A A D O E F L C C W C I G E O D
L N W S B X I V F R X Y I I S N L S O H
Y S I D C T C M E N W F L L A D Y I B K
M I L W S T P C L Y J W P D R I Y G G F
S V D P Y L U M C E O F M E C G W N E D
V E E J F R T F Q C S Q O R A N Q E L V
L W R D R Y S G L F Y S C D S A X D I V
R O I I T F A R M I R W L L M N K L T W
O W N O N C H A L A N T L Y V T C Y E D
P G G E N G G S S Y K C L X Q I T D E V
U W P J D F A P R X D E H H V I T G H P
T S S L X P C E R Z R K P I P R R A W G
S L O U C H E D W A T N E T N O C J L Y
R U E F U L L Y R A S S E T G G Q C F V
```

a select body, the best (5)
afraid, suspicious (12)
amazed, stupefied (6)
an ungainly gait (8)
beesechingly (11)
betraying fear, pain or surprise with an involuntary gesture (9)
bitter cutting jest (7)
by oneself (5)
compassion for suffering (4)
confused, perplexed (11)
confusedly (11)
cotton fabric shirt usually brightly colored (6)
deciding (8)
discharged completely, set free from a legal charge (9)
disgusted, anger with contempt (9)
driven to take any risk (9)
escaped, avoided (6)
essential, necessary to life (5)
giving up, accepting the future (10)
gloomily, somber (8)
heroic acts, adventures (8)
indifferently (12)

involved, complex (11)
likeness, similarity (11)
not fully awake (6)
regretfully, sorrowfully (8)
returning, repeatedly (9)
satisfied, pleased (7)
selling alcohol where not legally available (11)
senses are deadened (6)
suddenly (8)
swallow with greediness (6)
swerved, turned aside from a course or direction (6)
to shrink back as if from pain (6)
tuft of hair growing in a different direction (7)
uncommon, infrequent (6)
understood (7)
unwillingly, struggling (11)
wary, suspicious (5)
without direction, without purpose (9)
worth (5)

The Outsiders Vocabulary Word Search 2 Answer Key

```
R E S E M B L A N C E D E B A T I N G
E W S U L L E N L Y     C B G M   N
L A I   U       S     Q   R R P   I
U P   N   D   P     U     U O L   G
C P     C     E M   I E D   P G O G
T R       E R A D T X E E   T G R E
A E       A D   T P R   T B L Y I L
N H B   T R   E L E     A E Y K N R T
T E E E A A D O E       C W C I G E O
L N W S     I V   R     I I S N L S O
Y S I       T   M E     L L A D Y I B
  I L   S       C L   W P D R I   G
  V D       U     E O   M E C G   N E
  E E       R T F   C S   O R A N   E L
L   R   R   S G L     S C D S A   D I
R O I I     A R   I     L L M N   L T
O   N O N C H A L A N T L Y V T   Y E D
P G G E     G S   Y     C L   I T   E
U     D   A P R       E H     I T G
T           E     R       I   P R A
S L O U C H E D   A T N E T N O C   L
R U E F U L L Y R A S S E T G G
```

a select body, the best (5)
afraid, suspicious (12)
amazed, stupefied (6)
an ungainly gait (8)
beesechingly (11)
betraying fear, pain or surprise with an
  involuntary gesture (9)
bitter cutting jest (7)
by oneself (5)
compassion for suffering (4)
confused, perplexed (11)
confusedly (11)
cotton fabric shirt usually brightly colored (6)
deciding (8)
discharged completely, set free from a legal
  charge (9)
disgusted, anger with contempt (9)
driven to take any risk (9)
escaped, avoided (6)
essential, necessary to life (5)
giving up, accepting the future (10)
gloomily, somber (8)
heroic acts, adventures (8)
indifferently (12)

involved, complex (11)
likeness, similarity (11)
not fully awake (6)
regretfully, sorrowfully (8)
returning, repeatedly (9)
satisfied, pleased (7)
selling alcohol where not legally available (11)
senses are deadened (6)
suddenly (8)
swallow with greediness (6)
swerved, turned aside from a course or
  direction (6)
to shrink back as if from pain (6)
tuft of hair growing in a different direction (7)
uncommon, infrequent (6)
understood (7)
unwillingly, struggling (11)
wary, suspicious (5)
without direction, without purpose (9)
worth (5)

The Outsiders Vocabulary Word Search 3

```
E L U D E D E L I T E S L O U C H E D M
V C C E E D R K W B P S C Z G J H E J R
I O O T J L W E F Q I R R O Z R T N N M
S N N A I T I S C Y T N U D W T O J Y Y
N T V C T N Y R M U Y D G E I L Y G D Y
E E I I S E C N I Y R N E U F L I E G X
H M C T P T X R F O I R Q B E U C C G Y
E P T S W N K W E K U C I R A N L S K R
R T I I H O W A C D A S A N I T U L E N
P U O H K C G I B D U R L W G L I L Y C
P O N P W H M J V H D L B R L K U N Q G
A U Z O A I G O R G E D O E H C J V G R
I S H S M Y L N S K Z R N U T Y T E C X
M L T T H Y J Y K F N L O A S F D E V X
L Y T W Z L X L H W Y S N Q F E E R J W
E D D T R D Y M L Z J T C M C X T E G Z
S E R P C E L G C P L L H N E V A D N D
S S W Q M N T B Q Y S W A M X P C B I F
L P N G Z G P B D V D L L S P X I L R S
Y E G V H I U T Y E B V A A L R L O E S
B R B I Y S R E P M L D N C O J P Q V X
L A T T C E B S E B E N T R I U M C I X
M T M A D R A S I N H A L A T I O N U G
Q E F L Q R E A O Z H G Y S S W C G Q N
Z B H Y G R F L I N C H I N G L E E R Y
```

ABRUPTLY
ACQUITTED
AGHAST
AIMLESSLY
APPREHENSIVE
ASSET
COMPLICATED
CONTEMPTUOUSLY
CONTENT
CONVICTION
COWLICK
DEBATING
DELIRIOUS
DESPERATE
ELITE

ELUDED
EXPLOITS
FLINCHING
GORGED
GRASPED
GROGGY
INCREDULOUS
INHALATION
LEERY
LONED
MADRAS
MIMICKING
NONCHALANTLY
PITY
QUIVERING

RARELY
RECURRING
RELUCTANTLY
RESEMBLANCE
RESIGNEDLY
RUEFULLY
SARCASM
SLOUCHED
SOPHISTICATED
STUPOR
SULLENLY
VEERED
VITAL
WINCED

The Outsiders Vocabulary Word Search 3 Answer Key

```
E L U D E D E L I T E   S L O U C H E D
V C C E E   R       P   C   G     E
I O O T   L   E     I R O   R T
S N N A I T   I C   T U   W T O
N T V C   N   R U D G E   I Y G D
E E I I   E C   I R N E U F L I E G
H M C T   T   R   O I R Q B E U C C   Y
E P T S   N   E K U C I R A N L S K R
R T I I   O   A C D A S N I T U L E
P U O H   C G I   U R   W G L I L Y
P O N P   H M           L   L   U N
A U   O A I G O R G E D O E   C   V G
I S   S M               N U T     E
M L T       Y           L O A S   D E
L Y         L         Y   N     E R
E D         D Y         T C   C T E G
S E         E L           H N E A D N
S S         N T   Y       A M X C   I
L P         G P       D L L S P I   R
Y E     V   I U T   E B   A A   L O E
  R     I   S R E P M   D N C   O P V
  A     T   E B S E   E   T R I U M I
  T M A D R A S I N H A L A T I O N U
  E     L   R E A O       Y S S   C Q
            G R F L I N C H I N G L E E R Y
```

ABRUPTLY	ELUDED	RARELY
ACQUITTED	EXPLOITS	RECURRING
AGHAST	FLINCHING	RELUCTANTLY
AIMLESSLY	GORGED	RESEMBLANCE
APPREHENSIVE	GRASPED	RESIGNEDLY
ASSET	GROGGY	RUEFULLY
COMPLICATED	INCREDULOUS	SARCASM
CONTEMPTUOUSLY	INHALATION	SLOUCHED
CONTENT	LEERY	SOPHISTICATED
CONVICTION	LONED	STUPOR
COWLICK	MADRAS	SULLENLY
DEBATING	MIMICKING	VEERED
DELIRIOUS	NONCHALANTLY	VITAL
DESPERATE	PITY	WINCED
ELITE	QUIVERING	

The Outsiders Vocabulary Word Search 4

```
C P Z Q M R Y A R E L U C T A N T L Y G
O R N U I E G B P F X L D C S X A L R B
N E B I M S Q R T P E L R D W T G Y E R
V M C V I E K U O L R Z Z B I N L G E C
I O O E C M F P I G B E T V I D N S L G
C N W R K B W T S H G N H R R I I S L R
T I L I I L E L X Y A Y O E R G U Q E L
I T I N N A Z Y D N M L D R N O D X Y T
O I C G G N R T G N P L U E I S P M T G
N O K P P C V I V M I C D R F L I F C J
V N K N Z E D Q I W E L I C O K I V T K
D O S I Y N T S E R Y L E I T B N X E R
L N Q N I S M B H Y E D T G N L C X L P
Y C Y H X S L G Y D F S A N H V R G T J
M H K A V L Y O R Y T C R I T G E N Y Q
V A G L F C A S U A K X E T B O D I L D
G L T A F L T S S C S P P A Q R U R L V
G A Q T S U Z H S P H P S B R G L E U J
R N G I P U J Y W E S E E E L E O D F N
Y T C O M P L I C A T E D D E D U L E N
X L R N H E H L R W Q E E Q E K S I U T
X Y R N R M V C E Y C R R N G Q P W R L
A G H A S T A J T N E H O C O N T E N T
D H R W S S W I I E L L X V P S V B C W
D W Z D M L P W V C Z Y M A D R A S R C
```

ABRUPTLY	DELIRIOUS	INHALATION	RELUCTANTLY
AGHAST	DESPERATE	LEERY	RESEMBLANCE
APPREHENSIVE	ELITE	LONED	RESIGNEDLY
ASSET	ELUDED	MADRAS	RUEFULLY
BEWILDERDLY	EXPLOITS	MIMICKING	SARCASM
BEWILDERING	GORGED	NONCHALANTLY	SLOUCHED
COMPLICATED	GRASPED	PITY	STUPOR
CONTENT	GROGGY	PREMONITION	SULLENLY
CONVICTION	IMPLORINGLY	QUIVERING	VEERED
COWLICK	INCREDULOUS	RARELY	VITAL
DEBATING	INDIGNANT	RECURRING	WINCED

The Outsiders Vocabulary Word Search 4 Answer Key

```
C  P        Q  M     R        A  R  E  L  U  C  T  A  N  T  L  Y
O  R        U  I     E  G  B  P                       A  L  R
N  E        I  M     S     R     P  E              T  G  Y  E  R
V  M  C     V  I     E     U  O  L  R           I  N  L  G  E
I  O  O     E  C     M     P  I  G     E  T  V  I  D  N  S  L
C  N  W     R  K     B     T        G  N  H  R  R  I  I  S
T  I  L     I  I     L  E  L        A  Y  O  E  R  G  U     E
I  T  I     N  N        Y     N        L  D  R  N  O     X
O  I  C     G  G     N        G     P  U  E  I  S  P
N  O  K           C           I     M  I  C  D  R     L  I
   N              E  D        W  E  L  I        O     I  V
   O                 N           E  R  Y  L  E  I        N     E
   N           I     S     B           E     T  G        C
   C           N  J        L  G     D     S  A  N        R  G
   H           H           O  R              R  I     G  E  N  Y
   A           A        A  S  U        A    E  T     O  D  I  L
   L           L        T  S     C  S        P  A    R  U  R  L
   A           T  S  U        S           H  P  S  B  G  L  E  U
   N              I  P  U  Y     S  E  S  E  E  E     E  O     F
   T           C  O  M  P  L  I  C  A  T  E  D  D  E  D  U  L  E
   L        R  N        E     L  R           E  E     S  I     U
   Y              R        C  E  Y  C  R        N        W     R
A  G  H  A  S  T        A     T  N  E        O  C  O  N  T  E  N  T
      R              S  S        I  E  L                    B
                  M        P  W  V        Y  M  A  D  R  A  S
```

ABRUPTLY	DELIRIOUS	INHALATION	RELUCTANTLY
AGHAST	DESPERATE	LEERY	RESEMBLANCE
APPREHENSIVE	ELITE	LONED	RESIGNEDLY
ASSET	ELUDED	MADRAS	RUEFULLY
BEWILDERDLY	EXPLOITS	MIMICKING	SARCASM
BEWILDERING	GORGED	NONCHALANTLY	SLOUCHED
COMPLICATED	GRASPED	PITY	STUPOR
CONTENT	GROGGY	PREMONITION	SULLENLY
CONVICTION	IMPLORINGLY	QUIVERING	VEERED
COWLICK	INCREDULOUS	RARELY	VITAL
DEBATING	INDIGNANT	RECURRING	WINCED

The Outsiders Vocabulary Crossword 1

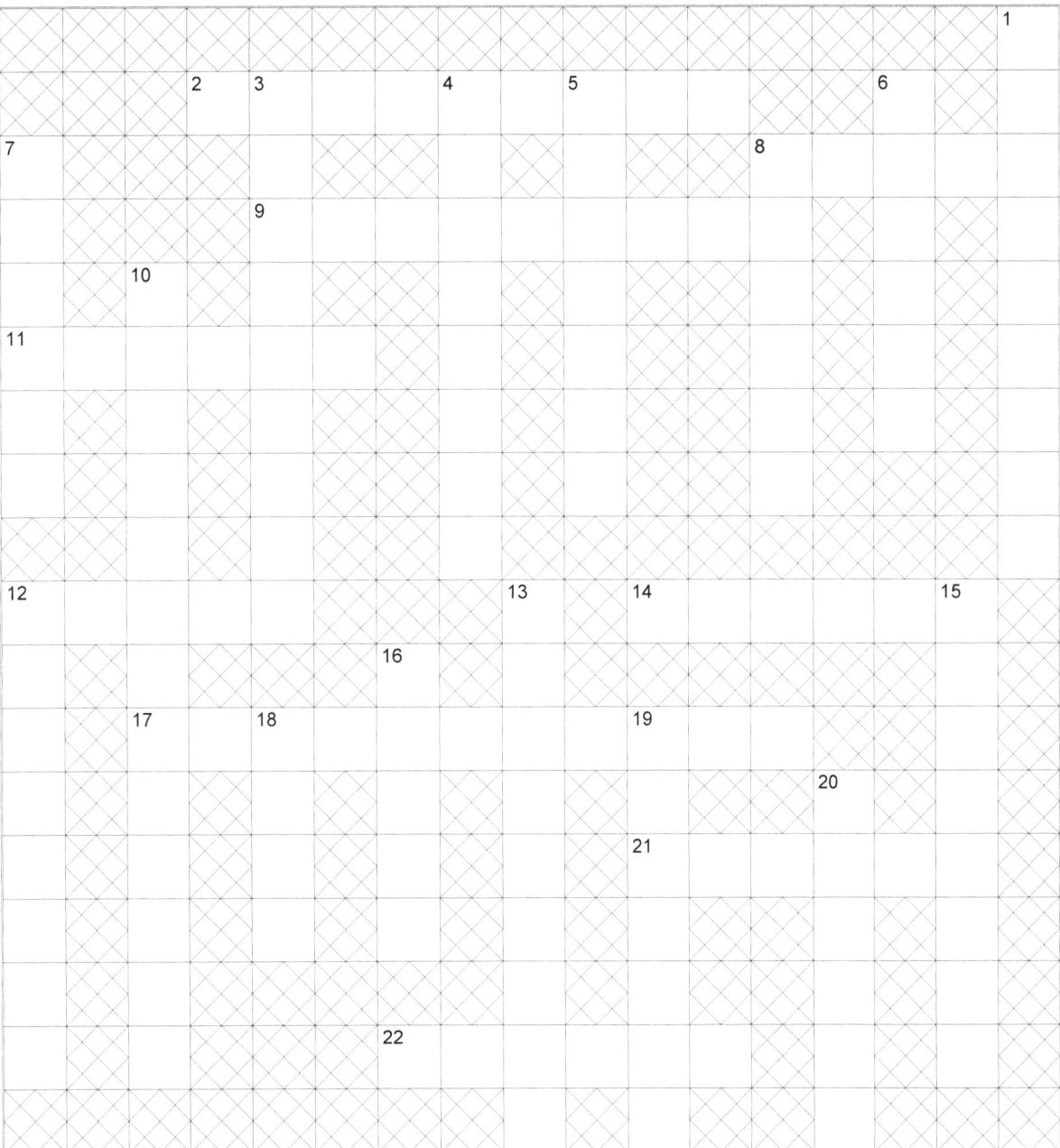

Across
2. without direction, without purpose
8. essential, necessary to life
9. driven to take any risk
11. not fully awake
12. worth
14. escaped, avoided
17. beesechingly
21. amazed, stupefied
22. to shrink back as if from pain

Down
1. confusion, disordered speech, hallucinations
3. disgusted, anger with contempt
4. heroic acts, adventures
5. bitter cutting jest
6. senses are deadened
7. swallow with greediness
8. swerved, turned aside from a course or direction
10. cultured, worldly
12. suddenly
13. trembling, shaking
15. deciding
16. by oneself
18. compassion for suffering
19. understood
20. uncommon, infrequent

The Outsiders Vocabulary Crossword 1 Answer Key

													¹D
			²A	³I	M	L	⁴E	S	⁵S	L	Y	⁶S	E
⁷G				N		X			A		⁸V	I	T	A	L
O				⁹D	E	S	P	E	R	A	T	E		U		I
R		¹⁰S		I		L		C		E		P		R
¹¹G	R	O	G	G	Y		O		A		R		O		I
E		P		N			I		S		E		R		O
D		H		A			T		M		D				U
		I		N			S								S
¹²A	S	S	E	T			¹³Q		¹⁴E	L	U	D	E	¹⁵D
B		T				¹⁶L		U						E
R		¹⁷I	M	¹⁸P	L	O	R	I	¹⁹N	G	L	Y		B
U		C		I		N		V		R			²⁰R		A
P		A		T		E		E		²¹A	G	H	A	S	T
T		T		Y		D		R		S			R		I
L		E						I		P			E		N
Y		D				²²W	I	N	C	E	D		L		G
								G		D			Y		

Across
2. without direction, without purpose
8. essential, necessary to life
9. driven to take any risk
11. not fully awake
12. worth
14. escaped, avoided
17. beesechingly
21. amazed, stupefied
22. to shrink back as if from pain

Down
1. confusion, disordered speech, hallucinations
3. disgusted, anger with contempt
4. heroic acts, adventures
5. bitter cutting jest
6. senses are deadened
7. swallow with greediness
8. swerved, turned aside from a course or direction
10. cultured, worldly
12. suddenly
13. trembling, shaking
15. deciding
16. by oneself
18. compassion for suffering
19. understood
20. uncommon, infrequent

The Outsiders Vocabulary Crossword 2

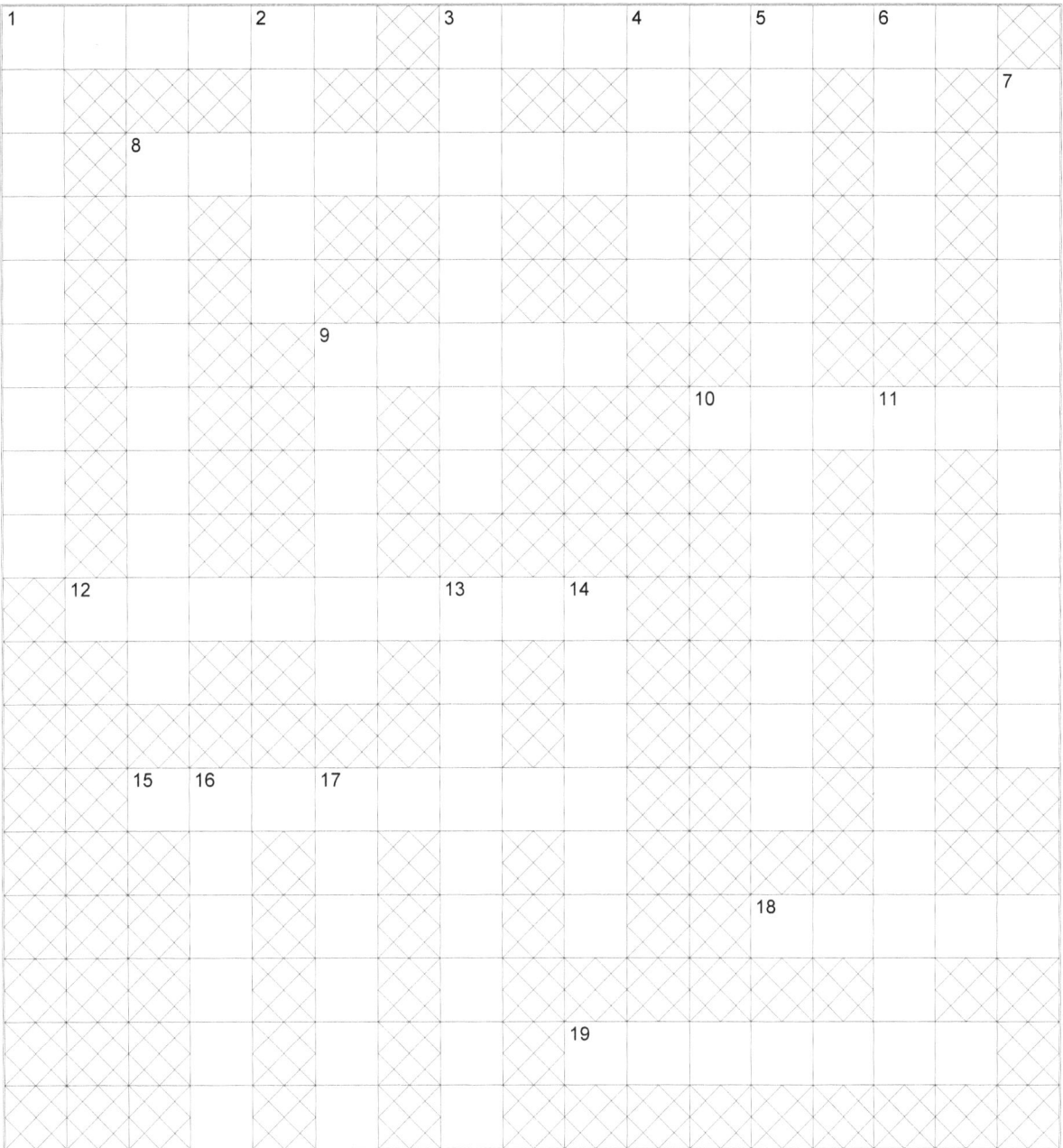

Across
1. cotton fabric shirt usually brightly colored
3. without direction, without purpose
8. driven to take any risk
9. essential, necessary to life
10. senses are deadened
12. trembling, shaking
15. deciding
18. a select body, the best
19. satisfied, pleased

Down
1. imitating, ridiculing
2. worth
3. suddenly
4. wary, suspicious
5. cultured, worldly
6. by oneself
7. beesechingly
8. confusion, disordered speech, hallucinations
9. swerved, turned aside from a course or direction
11. previous warning, information, feeling
13. disgusted, anger with contempt
14. swallow with greediness
16. escaped, avoided
17. amazed, stupefied

The Outsiders Vocabulary Crossword 2 Answer Key

	1 M	A	D	2 R	A	S		3 A	I	4 M	L	5 E	S	6 S	L	Y	
	I			S				B		E		O		O			7 I
	M		8 D	E	S	P	E	R	A	T	E			P		N		M
	I		E		S			U		R		H		E		P
	C		L		T			P		Y		I		D		L
	K		I			9 V	I	T	A	L		S				O
	I		R			E		L					10 S	T	U	11 P	O	R
	N		I			E		Y					I			R		I
	G		O			R							C			E		N
		12 Q	U	I	V	E	R	13 I	N	14 G			A			M		G
			S			D		N		O			T			O		L
								D		R			E			N		Y
			15 D	16 E	B	17 A	T	I	N	G			D			I
				L		G		G		E						T
				U		H		N		D			18 E	L	I	T	E
				D		A		A								O
				E		S		19 N		C	O	N	T	E	N	T
				D		T		T								

Across
1. cotton fabric shirt usually brightly colored
3. without direction, without purpose
8. driven to take any risk
9. essential, necessary to life
10. senses are deadened
12. trembling, shaking
15. deciding
18. a select body, the best
19. satisfied, pleased

Down
1. imitating, ridiculing
2. worth
3. suddenly
4. wary, suspicious
5. cultured, worldly
6. by oneself
7. beesechingly
8. confusion, disordered speech, hallucinations
9. swerved, turned aside from a course or direction
11. previous warning, information, feeling
13. disgusted, anger with contempt
14. swallow with greediness
16. escaped, avoided
17. amazed, stupefied

The Outsiders Vocabulary Crossword 3

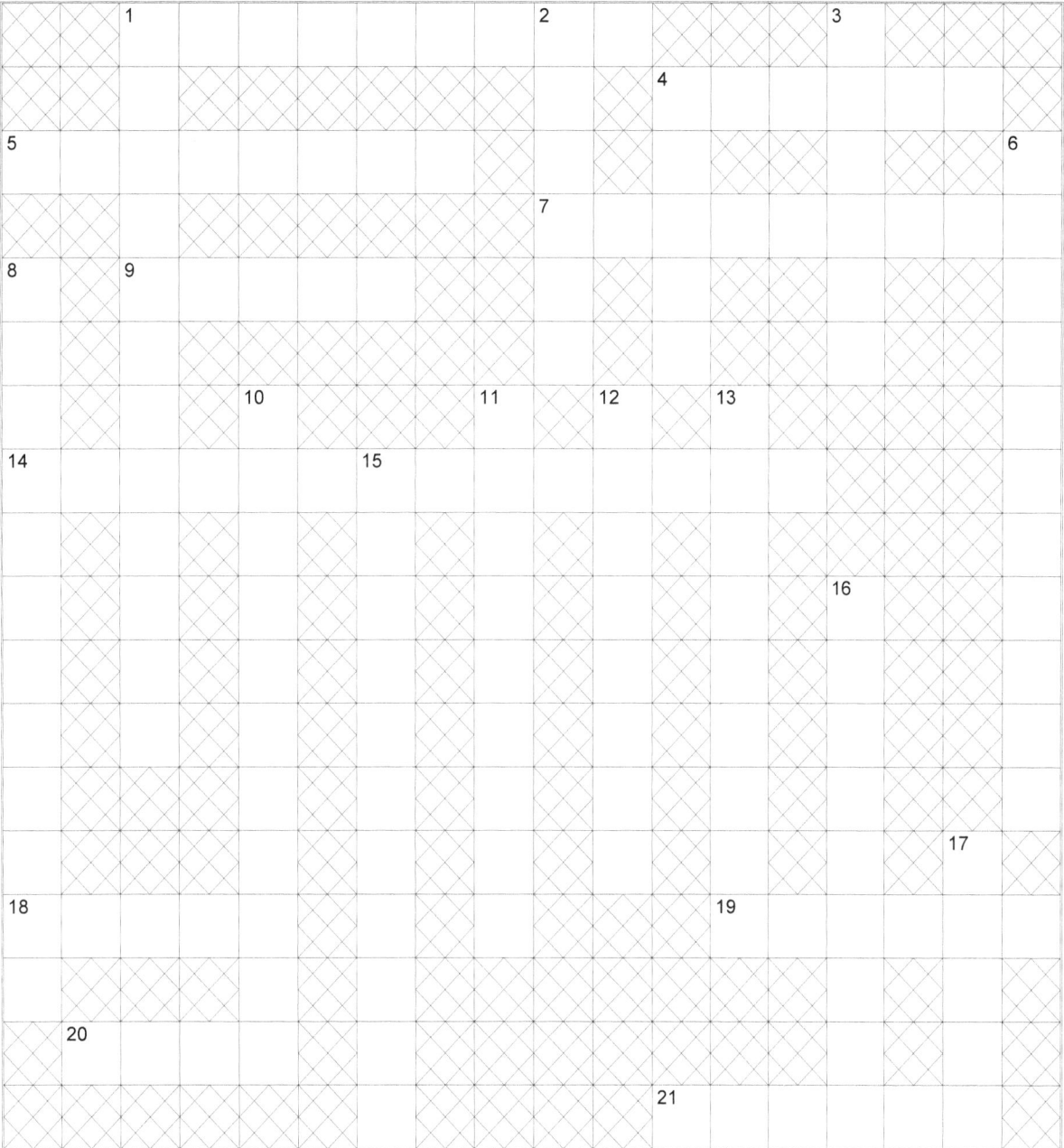

Across
1. discharged completely, set free from a legal charge
4. amazed, stupefied
5. heroic acts, adventures
7. driven to take any risk
9. a select body, the best
14. scornful, insolent
18. by oneself
19. swallow with greediness
20. compassion for suffering
21. not fully awake

Down
1. afraid, suspicious
2. escaped, avoided
3. cotton fabric shirt usually brightly colored
4. worth
6. likeness, similarity
8. indifferently
10. confusedly
11. trembling, shaking
12. regretfully, sorrowfully
13. betraying fear, pain or surprise with an involuntary gesture
15. previous warning, information, feeling
16. returning, repeatedly
17. wary, suspicious

The Outsiders Vocabulary Crossword 3 Answer Key

		1 A	C	Q	U	I	T	T	2 E	D			3 M			
		P							L		4 A	G	H	A	S	T
5 E	X	P	L	O	I	T	S		U		S		D			6 R
		R						7 D	E	S	P	E	R	A	T	E
8 N	9 E	L	I	T	E			E		E			A			S
O	H							D		T			S			E
N	E		10 B		11 Q		12 R		13 F				M	
14 C	O	N	T	E	M	15 P	T	U	O	U	S	L	Y			B
H		S		W		R		I		E		I				L
A		I		I		E		V		F		N		16 R		A
L		V		L		M		E		U		C		E		N
A		E		D		O		R		L		H		C		C
N				E		N		I		L		I		U		E
T				R		I		N		Y		N		R		17 L
18 L	O	N	E	D		T		G				19 G	O	R	G	E	D
Y						I								I		E
		20 P	I	T	Y		O							N		R
						N				21 G	R	O	G	G	Y

Across
1. discharged completely, set free from a legal charge
4. amazed, stupefied
5. heroic acts, adventures
7. driven to take any risk
9. a select body, the best
14. scornful, insolent
18. by oneself
19. swallow with greediness
20. compassion for suffering
21. not fully awake

Down
1. afraid, suspicious
2. escaped, avoided
3. cotton fabric shirt usually brightly colored
4. worth
6. likeness, similarity
8. indifferently
10. confusedly
11. trembling, shaking
12. regretfully, sorrowfully
13. betraying fear, pain or surprise with an involuntary gesture
15. previous warning, information, feeling
16. returning, repeatedly
17. wary, suspicious

The Outsiders Vocabulary Crossword 4

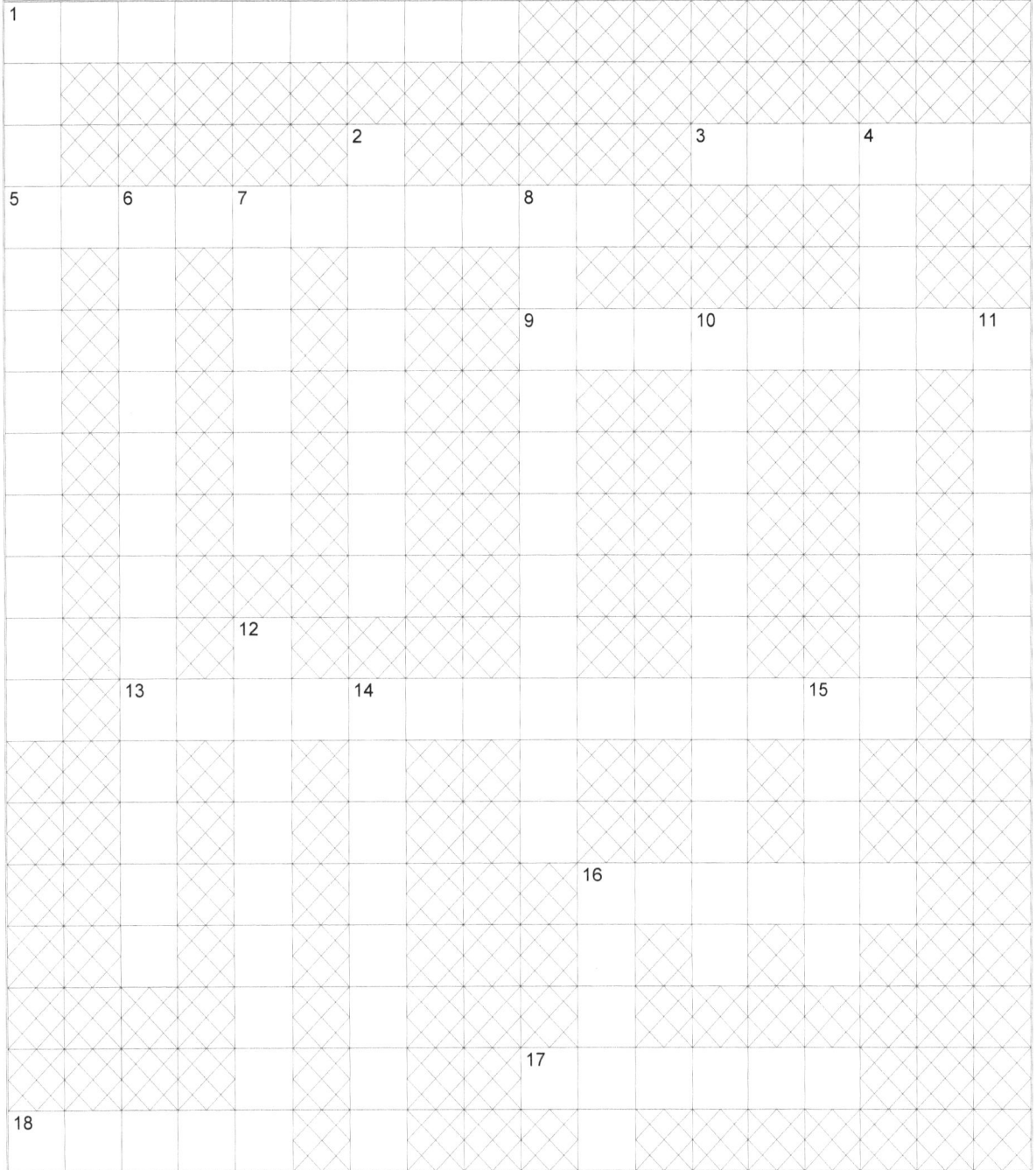

Across
1. discharged completely, set free from a legal charge
3. swerved, turned aside from a course or direction
5. likeness, similarity
9. imitating, ridiculing
13. scornful, insolent
16. escaped, avoided
17. senses are deadened
18. worth

Down
1. afraid, suspicious
2. an ungainly gait
4. giving up, accepting the future
6. cultured, worldly
7. cotton fabric shirt usually brightly colored
8. involved, complex
10. unbelieving
11. understood
12. disgusted, anger with contempt
14. heroic acts, adventures
15. by oneself
16. a select body, the best

The Outsiders Vocabulary Crossword 4 Answer Key

Across
1. discharged completely, set free from a legal charge
3. swerved, turned aside from a course or direction
5. likeness, similarity
9. imitating, ridiculing
13. scornful, insolent
16. escaped, avoided
17. senses are deadened
18. worth

Down
1. afraid, suspicious
2. an ungainly gait
4. giving up, accepting the future
6. cultured, worldly
7. cotton fabric shirt usually brightly colored
8. involved, complex
10. unbelieving
11. understood
12. disgusted, anger with contempt
14. heroic acts, adventures
15. by oneself
16. a select body, the best

The Outsiders Vocabulary Juggle Letters 1

1. CCOLIKW = 1. _____
   tuft of hair growing in a different direction

2. MYLAELISS = 2. _____
   without direction, without purpose

3. UEDDLE = 3. _____
   escaped, avoided

4. NTNIINADG = 4. _____
   disgusted, anger with contempt

5. OGYRGG = 5. _____
   not fully awake

6. YNILDEESRG = 6. _____
   giving up, accepting the future

7. NNAOYNLCLHAT = 7. _____
   indifferently

8. NLNCGIIFH = 8. _____
   betraying fear, pain or surprise with an involuntary gesture

9. NTSOMUOTEYPCUL = 9. _____
   scornful, insolent

10. OENTNTC = 10. _____
    satisfied, pleased

11. OCNCITNOVI = 11. _____
    strong belief

12. ACCOIEPLTMD = 12. _____
    involved, complex

13. AARSDM = 13. _____
    cotton fabric shirt usually brightly colored

14. RDGSAEP = 14. _____
    understood

15. TILOPEXS = 15. _____
    heroic acts, adventures

The Outsiders Vocabulary Juggle Letters 1 Answer Key

1. CCOLIKW = 1. COWLICK
   tuft of hair growing in a different direction

2. MYLAELISS = 2. AIMLESSLY
   without direction, without purpose

3. UEDDLE = 3. ELUDED
   escaped, avoided

4. NTNIINADG = 4. INDIGNANT
   disgusted, anger with contempt

5. OGYRGG = 5. GROGGY
   not fully awake

6. YNILDEESRG = 6. RESIGNEDLY
   giving up, accepting the future

7. NNAOYNLCLHAT = 7. NONCHALANTLY
   indifferently

8. NLNCGIIFH = 8. FLINCHING
   betraying fear, pain or surprise with an involuntary gesture

9. NTSOMUOTEYPCUL = 9. CONTEMPTUOUSLY
   scornful, insolent

10. OENTNTC =10. CONTENT
    satisfied, pleased

11. OCNCITNOVI =11. CONVICTION
    strong belief

12. ACCOIEPLTMD =12. COMPLICATED
    involved, complex

13. AARSDM =13. MADRAS
    cotton fabric shirt usually brightly colored

14. RDGSAEP =14. GRASPED
    understood

15. TILOPEXS =15. EXPLOITS
    heroic acts, adventures

The Outsiders Vocabulary Juggle Letters 2

1. LDUDEE = 1. _____
   escaped, avoided

2. LRPUTYBA = 2. _____
   suddenly

3. AOLHTALYNNNC = 3. _____
   indifferently

4. CIMKIGNMI = 4. _____
   imitating, ridiculing

5. OSEASCHIPIDTT = 5. _____
   cultured, worldly

6. LOWCKIC = 6. _____
   tuft of hair growing in a different direction

7. GLDEESYRNI = 7. _____
   giving up, accepting the future

8. STEAS = 8. _____
   worth

9. LCCMDTAIEOP = 9. _____
   involved, complex

10. LURFUEYL = 10. _____
    regretfully, sorrowfully

11. ENODL = 11. _____
    by oneself

12. DPSGERA = 12. _____
    understood

13. AIVLT = 13. _____
    essential, necessary to life

14. ITNGNIDAN = 14. _____
    disgusted, anger with contempt

15. CONNCOITVI = 15. _____
    strong belief

The Outsiders Vocabulary Juggle Letters 2 Answer Key

1. LDUDEE = 1. ELUDED
   escaped, avoided

2. LRPUTYBA = 2. ABRUPTLY
   suddenly

3. AOLHTALYNNNC = 3. NONCHALANTLY
   indifferently

4. CIMKIGNMI = 4. MIMICKING
   imitating, ridiculing

5. OSEASCHIPIDTT = 5. SOPHISTICATED
   cultured, worldly

6. LOWCKIC = 6. COWLICK
   tuft of hair growing in a different direction

7. GLDEESYRNI = 7. RESIGNEDLY
   giving up, accepting the future

8. STEAS = 8. ASSET
   worth

9. LCCMDTAIEOP = 9. COMPLICATED
   involved, complex

10. LURFUEYL = 10. RUEFULLY
    regretfully, sorrowfully

11. ENODL = 11. LONED
    by oneself

12. DPSGERA = 12. GRASPED
    understood

13. AIVLT = 13. VITAL
    essential, necessary to life

14. ITNGNIDAN = 14. INDIGNANT
    disgusted, anger with contempt

15. CONNCOITVI = 15. CONVICTION
    strong belief

The Outsiders Vocabulary Juggle Letters 3

1. OSCEHULD = 1. _____
   an ungainly gait

2. GLGNGBEOTOI = 2. _____
   selling alcohol where not legally available

3. RGODEG = 3. _____
   swallow with greediness

4. ROPNOMTINEI = 4. _____
   previous warning, information, feeling

5. ELBWYIDLDRE = 5. _____
   confusedly

6. HLNINFCGI = 6. _____
   betraying fear, pain or surprise with an involuntary gesture

7. CSIUDOULREN = 7. _____
   unbelieving

8. MRAASD = 8. _____
   cotton fabric shirt usually brightly colored

9. ENEPRHAIVPES = 9. _____
   afraid, suspicious

10. NEIWCD = 10. _____
    to shrink back as if from pain

11. DAESGRP = 11. _____
    understood

12. ULELSLNY = 12. _____
    gloomily, somber

13. ACAMRSS = 13. _____
    bitter cutting jest

14. ASMLCERENBE = 14. _____
    likeness, similarity

15. IYTP = 15. _____
    compassion for suffering

The Outsiders Vocabulary Juggle Letters 3 Answer Key

1. OSCEHULD = 1. SLOUCHED
   an ungainly gait
2. GLGNGBEOTOI = 2. BOOTLEGGING
   selling alcohol where not legally available
3. RGODEG = 3. GORGED
   swallow with greediness
4. ROPNOMTINEI = 4. PREMONITION
   previous warning, information, feeling
5. ELBWYIDLDRE = 5. BEWILDERDLY
   confusedly
6. HLNINFCGI = 6. FLINCHING
   betraying fear, pain or surprise with an involuntary gesture
7. CSIUDOULREN = 7. INCREDULOUS
   unbelieving
8. MRAASD = 8. MADRAS
   cotton fabric shirt usually brightly colored
9. ENEPRHAIVPES = 9. APPREHENSIVE
   afraid, suspicious
10. NEIWCD = 10. WINCED
    to shrink back as if from pain
11. DAESGRP = 11. GRASPED
    understood
12. ULELSLNY = 12. SULLENLY
    gloomily, somber
13. ACAMRSS = 13. SARCASM
    bitter cutting jest
14. ASMLCERENBE = 14. RESEMBLANCE
    likeness, similarity
15. IYTP = 15. PITY
    compassion for suffering

The Outsiders Vocabulary Juggle Letters 4

1. IASLLSMYE = 1. _____
   without direction, without purpose

2. ARYELR = 2. _____
   uncommon, infrequent

3. ERIUGNCRR = 3. _____
   returning, repeatedly

4. ETUITCQDA = 4. _____
   discharged completely, set free from a legal charge

5. KIMICNIMG = 5. _____
   imitating, ridiculing

6. PDSEGRA = 6. _____
   understood

7. ATPEESRDE = 7. _____
   driven to take any risk

8. ULTEYTRNLAC = 8. _____
   unwillingly, struggling

9. DSHELOCU = 9. _____
   an ungainly gait

10. ECONTTN =10. _____
    satisfied, pleased

11. ANRLBEMSCEE =11. _____
    likeness, similarity

12. ELUYLFUR =12. _____
    regretfully, sorrowfully

13. EDEULD =13. _____
    escaped, avoided

14. NDINTNAIG =14. _____
    disgusted, anger with contempt

15. RNOTMIPONIE =15. _____
    previous warning, information, feeling

The Outsiders Vocabulary Juggle Letters 4 Answer Key

1. IASLLSMYE = 1. AIMLESSLY
   without direction, without purpose

2. ARYELR = 2. RARELY
   uncommon, infrequent

3. ERIUGNCRR = 3. RECURRING
   returning, repeatedly

4. ETUITCQDA = 4. ACQUITTED
   discharged completely, set free from a legal charge

5. KIMICNIMG = 5. MIMICKING
   imitating, ridiculing

6. PDSEGRA = 6. GRASPED
   understood

7. ATPEESRDE = 7. DESPERATE
   driven to take any risk

8. ULTEYTRNLAC = 8. RELUCTANTLY
   unwillingly, struggling

9. DSHELOCU = 9. SLOUCHED
   an ungainly gait

10. ECONTTN =10. CONTENT
    satisfied, pleased

11. ANRLBEMSCEE =11. RESEMBLANCE
    likeness, similarity

12. ELUYLFUR =12. RUEFULLY
    regretfully, sorrowfully

13. EDEULD =13. ELUDED
    escaped, avoided

14. NDINTNAIG =14. INDIGNANT
    disgusted, anger with contempt

15. RNOTMIPONIE =15. PREMONITION
    previous warning, information, feeling

ABRUPTLY	suddenly
ACQUITTED	discharged completely, set free from a legal charge
AGHAST	amazed, stupefied
AIMLESSLY	without direction, without purpose
APPREHENSIVE	afraid, suspicious
ASSET	worth

BEWILDERDLY	confusedly
BEWILDERING	confused, perplexed
BOOTLEGGING	selling alcohol where not legally available
COMPLICATED	involved, complex
CONTEMPTUOUSLY	scornful, insolent
CONTENT	satisfied, pleased

CONVICTION	strong belief
COWLICK	tuft of hair growing in a different direction
DEBATING	deciding
DELIRIOUS	confusion, disordered speech, hallucinations
DESPERATE	driven to take any risk
ELITE	a select body, the best

ELUDED	escaped, avoided
EXPLOITS	heroic acts, adventures
FLINCHING	betraying fear, pain or surprise with an involuntary gesture
GORGED	swallow with greediness
GRASPED	understood
GROGGY	not fully awake

IMPLORINGLY	beesechingly
INCREDULOUS	unbelieving
INDIGNANT	disgusted, anger with contempt
INHALATION	to breathe into the lungs
LEERY	wary, suspicious
LONED	by oneself

MADRAS	cotton fabric shirt usually brightly colored
MIMICKING	imitating, ridiculing
NONCHALANTLY	indifferently
PITY	compassion for suffering
PREMONITION	previous warning, information, feeling
QUIVERING	trembling, shaking

RARELY	uncommon, infrequent
RECURRING	returning, repeatedly
RELUCTANTLY	unwillingly, struggling
RESEMBLANCE	likeness, similarity
RESIGNEDLY	giving up, accepting the future
RUEFULLY	regretfully, sorrowfully

SARCASM	bitter cutting jest
SLOUCHED	an ungainly gait
SOPHISTICATED	cultured, worldly
STUPOR	senses are deadened
SULLENLY	gloomily, somber
VEERED	swerved, turned aside from a course or direction

VITAL	essential, necessary to life
WINCED	to shrink back as if from pain

The Outsiders Vocabulary

RARELY	NONCHALANTLY	RESIGNEDLY	ACQUITTED	AIMLESSLY
IMPLORINGLY	ELITE	DELIRIOUS	COWLICK	CONTEMPTUOUSLY
PREMONITION	RECURRING	FREE SPACE	WINCED	LEERY
CONVICTION	GROGGY	EXPLOITS	SULLENLY	ASSET
CONTENT	DESPERATE	BEWILDERDLY	ELUDED	VEERED

The Outsiders Vocabulary

LONED	GRASPED	BOOTLEGGING	GORGED	PITY
RELUCTANTLY	RUEFULLY	SLOUCHED	MIMICKING	MADRAS
ABRUPTLY	INHALATION	FREE SPACE	QUIVERING	DEBATING
FLINCHING	RESEMBLANCE	APPREHENSIVE	AGHAST	INCREDULOUS
COMPLICATED	VITAL	SOPHISTICATED	SARCASM	BEWILDERING

The Outsiders Vocabulary

SLOUCHED	RUEFULLY	IMPLORINGLY	INHALATION	CONTEMPTUOUSLY
DELIRIOUS	GORGED	SULLENLY	APPREHENSIVE	BEWILDERDLY
ELITE	RESIGNEDLY	FREE SPACE	INCREDULOUS	DEBATING
STUPOR	SOPHISTICATED	INDIGNANT	RARELY	EXPLOITS
BEWILDERING	WINCED	GROGGY	PREMONITION	ACQUITTED

The Outsiders Vocabulary

MIMICKING	QUIVERING	AGHAST	ASSET	GRASPED
PITY	LEERY	FLINCHING	CONVICTION	DESPERATE
RECURRING	CONTENT	FREE SPACE	AIMLESSLY	ABRUPTLY
RESEMBLANCE	NONCHALANTLY	VITAL	COMPLICATED	LONED
SARCASM	COWLICK	MADRAS	BOOTLEGGING	VEERED

The Outsiders Vocabulary

RESIGNEDLY	EXPLOITS	DESPERATE	QUIVERING	GRASPED
ACQUITTED	BEWILDERING	CONVICTION	CONTENT	AGHAST
CONTEMPTUOUSLY	RUEFULLY	FREE SPACE	APPREHENSIVE	LONED
STUPOR	PITY	SOPHISTICATED	ASSET	VEERED
MIMICKING	VITAL	PREMONITION	ABRUPTLY	RARELY

The Outsiders Vocabulary

COWLICK	FLINCHING	RELUCTANTLY	BEWILDERDLY	SULLENLY
GORGED	INHALATION	SARCASM	LEERY	MADRAS
ELUDED	GROGGY	FREE SPACE	INDIGNANT	DEBATING
INCREDULOUS	RECURRING	IMPLORINGLY	SLOUCHED	RESEMBLANCE
WINCED	DELIRIOUS	COMPLICATED	BOOTLEGGING	NONCHALANTLY

The Outsiders Vocabulary

QUIVERING	BEWILDERING	RESEMBLANCE	SLOUCHED	PREMONITION
AGHAST	STUPOR	ASSET	ELUDED	INDIGNANT
MIMICKING	RARELY	FREE SPACE	SARCASM	ACQUITTED
LONED	GORGED	MADRAS	BOOTLEGGING	VEERED
BEWILDERDLY	RESIGNEDLY	COMPLICATED	SULLENLY	ELITE

The Outsiders Vocabulary

DESPERATE	EXPLOITS	CONTENT	COWLICK	IMPLORINGLY
APPREHENSIVE	FLINCHING	WINCED	CONVICTION	PITY
ABRUPTLY	INCREDULOUS	FREE SPACE	RUEFULLY	SOPHISTICATED
GROGGY	GRASPED	INHALATION	VITAL	LEERY
DEBATING	RECURRING	NONCHALANTLY	AIMLESSLY	CONTEMPTUOUSLY

The Outsiders Vocabulary

FLINCHING	RESEMBLANCE	IMPLORINGLY	DEBATING	RESIGNEDLY
GRASPED	CONVICTION	ASSET	RUEFULLY	RELUCTANTLY
WINCED	PREMONITION	FREE SPACE	VEERED	LONED
INDIGNANT	DESPERATE	SOPHISTICATED	ELUDED	BOOTLEGGING
CONTEMPTUOUSLY	MIMICKING	RARELY	BEWILDERDLY	AGHAST

The Outsiders Vocabulary

EXPLOITS	COMPLICATED	ACQUITTED	SULLENLY	QUIVERING
INCREDULOUS	ELITE	MADRAS	AIMLESSLY	SLOUCHED
COWLICK	NONCHALANTLY	FREE SPACE	DELIRIOUS	RECURRING
APPREHENSIVE	INHALATION	CONTENT	PITY	ABRUPTLY
GROGGY	STUPOR	BEWILDERING	VITAL	SARCASM

The Outsiders Vocabulary

INHALATION	PREMONITION	COMPLICATED	DEBATING	DELIRIOUS
MIMICKING	EXPLOITS	ABRUPTLY	BEWILDERDLY	AGHAST
RECURRING	ASSET	FREE SPACE	LEERY	SLOUCHED
QUIVERING	SULLENLY	CONTEMPTUOUSLY	DESPERATE	RUEFULLY
BOOTLEGGING	PITY	INCREDULOUS	RARELY	AIMLESSLY

The Outsiders Vocabulary

RESEMBLANCE	CONTENT	ACQUITTED	RELUCTANTLY	RESIGNEDLY
BEWILDERING	GRASPED	IMPLORINGLY	GROGGY	VEERED
MADRAS	SOPHISTICATED	FREE SPACE	GORGED	SARCASM
NONCHALANTLY	WINCED	ELUDED	INDIGNANT	STUPOR
VITAL	APPREHENSIVE	CONVICTION	FLINCHING	COWLICK

The Outsiders Vocabulary

INDIGNANT	DELIRIOUS	DESPERATE	RESEMBLANCE	GRASPED
BOOTLEGGING	ACQUITTED	GROGGY	PREMONITION	COMPLICATED
LONED	VITAL	FREE SPACE	DEBATING	CONTEMPTUOUSLY
APPREHENSIVE	SOPHISTICATED	ABRUPTLY	QUIVERING	EXPLOITS
ASSET	SARCASM	AIMLESSLY	MADRAS	RELUCTANTLY

The Outsiders Vocabulary

INHALATION	SLOUCHED	LEERY	WINCED	ELITE
NONCHALANTLY	CONVICTION	BEWILDERING	SULLENLY	ELUDED
FLINCHING	RARELY	FREE SPACE	MIMICKING	CONTENT
RESIGNEDLY	AGHAST	GORGED	STUPOR	RECURRING
PITY	IMPLORINGLY	INCREDULOUS	BEWILDERDLY	RUEFULLY

The Outsiders Vocabulary

CONTEMPTUOUSLY	VEERED	RELUCTANTLY	LEERY	DELIRIOUS
GRASPED	CONTENT	WINCED	INHALATION	MIMICKING
QUIVERING	SLOUCHED	FREE SPACE	SULLENLY	COWLICK
CONVICTION	BEWILDERDLY	SOPHISTICATED	AGHAST	PITY
ASSET	EXPLOITS	STUPOR	AIMLESSLY	RESEMBLANCE

The Outsiders Vocabulary

DESPERATE	RUEFULLY	INCREDULOUS	ABRUPTLY	DEBATING
APPREHENSIVE	INDIGNANT	SARCASM	COMPLICATED	ELUDED
ELITE	BOOTLEGGING	FREE SPACE	MADRAS	RARELY
NONCHALANTLY	FLINCHING	LONED	VITAL	RECURRING
ACQUITTED	BEWILDERING	RESIGNEDLY	GROGGY	PREMONITION

The Outsiders Vocabulary

NONCHALANTLY	PITY	EXPLOITS	CONVICTION	QUIVERING
DELIRIOUS	WINCED	MADRAS	MIMICKING	RELUCTANTLY
GROGGY	SLOUCHED	FREE SPACE	GORGED	SARCASM
ACQUITTED	INDIGNANT	LONED	AIMLESSLY	RUEFULLY
SULLENLY	RESEMBLANCE	VITAL	VEERED	COWLICK

The Outsiders Vocabulary

RECURRING	RESIGNEDLY	INHALATION	ABRUPTLY	AGHAST
ELUDED	CONTENT	PREMONITION	SOPHISTICATED	BOOTLEGGING
ELITE	DEBATING	FREE SPACE	FLINCHING	BEWILDERING
STUPOR	INCREDULOUS	GRASPED	APPREHENSIVE	IMPLORINGLY
BEWILDERDLY	COMPLICATED	RARELY	DESPERATE	ASSET

The Outsiders Vocabulary

MIMICKING	INDIGNANT	GRASPED	INHALATION	STUPOR
BOOTLEGGING	COWLICK	DESPERATE	CONTENT	PITY
APPREHENSIVE	VITAL	FREE SPACE	RELUCTANTLY	BEWILDERDLY
RECURRING	AGHAST	EXPLOITS	ASSET	CONVICTION
QUIVERING	RESEMBLANCE	DEBATING	FLINCHING	WINCED

The Outsiders Vocabulary

IMPLORINGLY	SARCASM	AIMLESSLY	SULLENLY	ELITE
LEERY	NONCHALANTLY	ACQUITTED	PREMONITION	GORGED
RESIGNEDLY	VEERED	FREE SPACE	DELIRIOUS	LONED
CONTEMPTUOUSLY	INCREDULOUS	COMPLICATED	SLOUCHED	MADRAS
BEWILDERING	RUEFULLY	SOPHISTICATED	ELUDED	GROGGY

The Outsiders Vocabulary

SULLENLY	GRASPED	CONTEMPTUOUSLY	CONTENT	NONCHALANTLY
COWLICK	GROGGY	RESIGNEDLY	INDIGNANT	LONED
PREMONITION	QUIVERING	FREE SPACE	IMPLORINGLY	RARELY
WINCED	INCREDULOUS	BEWILDERDLY	VITAL	AIMLESSLY
SOPHISTICATED	BEWILDERING	LEERY	SLOUCHED	RESEMBLANCE

The Outsiders Vocabulary

INHALATION	DEBATING	RUEFULLY	ELUDED	RELUCTANTLY
APPREHENSIVE	DESPERATE	STUPOR	FLINCHING	VEERED
ELITE	ABRUPTLY	FREE SPACE	EXPLOITS	ASSET
AGHAST	SARCASM	RECURRING	COMPLICATED	ACQUITTED
CONVICTION	PITY	GORGED	DELIRIOUS	BOOTLEGGING

The Outsiders Vocabulary

SULLENLY	SLOUCHED	STUPOR	COWLICK	CONVICTION
INHALATION	DELIRIOUS	BEWILDERING	INCREDULOUS	DEBATING
LONED	ABRUPTLY	FREE SPACE	CONTENT	DESPERATE
ELUDED	PITY	RESIGNEDLY	BEWILDERDLY	MIMICKING
VEERED	RECURRING	EXPLOITS	WINCED	INDIGNANT

The Outsiders Vocabulary

SARCASM	RELUCTANTLY	GROGGY	PREMONITION	NONCHALANTLY
QUIVERING	CONTEMPTUOUSLY	LEERY	MADRAS	RUEFULLY
RARELY	ACQUITTED	FREE SPACE	VITAL	ELITE
AIMLESSLY	AGHAST	COMPLICATED	GRASPED	RESEMBLANCE
IMPLORINGLY	FLINCHING	GORGED	BOOTLEGGING	ASSET

The Outsiders Vocabulary

ELUDED	APPREHENSIVE	VITAL	PITY	RUEFULLY
INHALATION	VEERED	LONED	RARELY	STUPOR
MADRAS	RESEMBLANCE	FREE SPACE	DELIRIOUS	QUIVERING
AGHAST	ACQUITTED	EXPLOITS	DEBATING	PREMONITION
MIMICKING	CONTEMPTUOUSLY	RELUCTANTLY	COMPLICATED	IMPLORINGLY

The Outsiders Vocabulary

ASSET	INDIGNANT	AIMLESSLY	NONCHALANTLY	BEWILDERING
ABRUPTLY	INCREDULOUS	GROGGY	CONVICTION	COWLICK
BEWILDERDLY	CONTENT	FREE SPACE	LEERY	WINCED
GORGED	RESIGNEDLY	BOOTLEGGING	RECURRING	SARCASM
ELITE	SOPHISTICATED	SLOUCHED	FLINCHING	DESPERATE

The Outsiders Vocabulary

VITAL	RUEFULLY	CONTEMPTUOUSLY	PREMONITION	AIMLESSLY
BEWILDERING	LONED	MIMICKING	ASSET	GROGGY
ACQUITTED	DEBATING	FREE SPACE	GORGED	ELUDED
GRASPED	QUIVERING	SARCASM	RESEMBLANCE	DELIRIOUS
APPREHENSIVE	WINCED	INCREDULOUS	STUPOR	MADRAS

The Outsiders Vocabulary

SOPHISTICATED	NONCHALANTLY	SULLENLY	ELITE	CONTENT
COMPLICATED	RARELY	VEERED	SLOUCHED	DESPERATE
BOOTLEGGING	BEWILDERDLY	FREE SPACE	CONVICTION	RECURRING
RELUCTANTLY	AGHAST	EXPLOITS	LEERY	IMPLORINGLY
INHALATION	ABRUPTLY	RESIGNEDLY	INDIGNANT	COWLICK

The Outsiders Vocabulary

GRASPED	APPREHENSIVE	ELITE	LONED	RUEFULLY
STUPOR	FLINCHING	COWLICK	MIMICKING	COMPLICATED
BEWILDERING	RESIGNEDLY	FREE SPACE	VITAL	SULLENLY
PITY	WINCED	SLOUCHED	RARELY	MADRAS
DEBATING	BOOTLEGGING	CONVICTION	LEERY	DESPERATE

The Outsiders Vocabulary

INCREDULOUS	EXPLOITS	AIMLESSLY	ASSET	ELUDED
INHALATION	ABRUPTLY	PREMONITION	GROGGY	NONCHALANTLY
VEERED	ACQUITTED	FREE SPACE	CONTENT	GORGED
RELUCTANTLY	SARCASM	SOPHISTICATED	AGHAST	CONTEMPTUOUSLY
INDIGNANT	BEWILDERDLY	IMPLORINGLY	RECURRING	QUIVERING

The Outsiders Vocabulary

RESEMBLANCE	MADRAS	RELUCTANTLY	VEERED	GORGED
APPREHENSIVE	DESPERATE	ELUDED	BEWILDERDLY	ELITE
SLOUCHED	INCREDULOUS	FREE SPACE	SOPHISTICATED	ASSET
FLINCHING	DELIRIOUS	COMPLICATED	CONTEMPTUOUSLY	LONED
STUPOR	SARCASM	RESIGNEDLY	PITY	DEBATING

The Outsiders Vocabulary

SULLENLY	GROGGY	CONVICTION	GRASPED	RUEFULLY
MIMICKING	CONTENT	VITAL	PREMONITION	NONCHALANTLY
BEWILDERING	QUIVERING	FREE SPACE	INDIGNANT	RECURRING
BOOTLEGGING	ACQUITTED	AGHAST	COWLICK	EXPLOITS
RARELY	WINCED	ABRUPTLY	LEERY	IMPLORINGLY